**visual communications international**

# visual communications: international

a report on the fifth communications conference
of the Art Directors Club of New York

FRANK BAKER, *editor*
EDWARD S. MORSE, *executive editor*
for the Art Directors Club of New York

Communication Arts Books, Hastings House, Publishers
New York 22

This book designed by Arthur Hawkins

The world-eye symbol by Matthew Basile

THE WHITE HOUSE
WASHINGTON, D.C.

April 13, 1960

Frank Baker, Director, Visual
Communications—International
Art Directors Club of New York

It is a pleasure to send greetings to
those attending the First
International Visual Communications
Conference sponsored by the Art
Directors Club of New York. By
means of visual communication,
much is being done to increase
understanding among the peoples of
the world. A broader teaching of the
arts, history, and traditions of
mankind is an essential part of the
building of peace.

I am delighted to add my best wishes
for a memorable conference.

DWIGHT D. EISENHOWER

# Contents

## Officers of the Art Directors Club of New York

Garrett P. Orr: President

Edward R. Wade: First Vice-President

A. Russell Hillier: Second Vice President

Andrew K. Nelsen: Secretary

Mahlon A. Cline: Treasurer

Stephen Baker

Louis Dorfsman

Ed Graham

George Krikorian

John A. Skidmore

William Strosahl


## Conference Committee

Frank Baker: Conference Director

Arthur Hawkins: Conference Chairman

Ed Graham: Executive Board Member

Gene Federico: Design Chairman

Matthew Basile: Conference Designer

Wallace W. Elton: Program Planning

Elwood Whitney: Program Planning

John Tinker: Program Planning

William Schneider: Program Planning

John Jamison: Finance

John A. Skidmore: Operations

Eugene Milbauer: Operations

William Duffy: Operations

Franc Ritter: Operations

Edward J. Bennett: Reception

Paul G. Lawler: Reception

Walter Grotz: Reception

Wallace W. Elton: Reception

Edward P. Diehl: Photography

Alton Ketchum: Associate Member

Gus Scheuer: Associate Member

Miss Marion Sheldon: Conference Secretary

Edward S. Morse: Publicity

GARRETT P. ORR
*President, the Art Directors
Club of New York*

In the conviction that recognition of the importance of the art director is in direct proportion to the growth in importance of the art of communicating through the eye, the Art Directors Club of New York in 1956 launched the First Annual Visual Communications Conference. These Conferences were conceived, not as isolated meetings of artists and art directors, but as a series of annual symposia which would provide continuing opportunity for a meeting of the minds between art directors and management.

The years ahead will bring to almost all industry an increasing number of foreign branches and working agreements, and an increasing amount of foreign commerce of all kinds. Advertising is going to be in the thick of this and will benefit in direct proportion to its ability to communicate.

With an awareness of the growing importance of the international aspect, the Art Directors Club chose as its theme for the 1960 Conference, its fifth, "Visual Communications—International."

**FRANK BAKER**
*Conference Director*

We believe that we have much to learn from each other—how our problems and solutions differ—how they are the same—how different is our thinking—the language problem—local customs—all the things that are the people of our world.

The Conference sought to identify the characteristics held in common by all peoples, determine the elements of difference, and then arrive at a common denominator for global communication.

We set forth this premise: "The differences in people are not as important as their samenesses."

We hope that the Conference, and this Conference Report, will prove to be a contribution to the advancement of understanding among nations.

**ARTHUR HAWKINS**
*Conference Chairman*

*Minding your own business is old fashioned. Whether you are a country or a person, isolation no longer pays off.*

*The era we are living in today is indelibly marked by the free interchange of ideas, the free exchange of views—in short, by communication.*

*Men of good will everywhere are in conference—bent on solving whatever problems they may now have or preparing themselves to overcome future difficulties.*

*In New York, in the Spring of 1960, creative people joined in conference for the fifth consecutive year. For two mornings and two afternoons they talked and demonstrated and listened and questioned—people from the north and south and east and west of America, and from England and Sweden and Italy and France, and from Germany and Brazil and Canada and India and Uruguay.*

*It has been our intention in this book to preserve some of the inspirational moments that came out of this thinking-man's meeting.*

# The End of "Modern Times"

## SYLVESTER L. (PAT) WEAVER

As chairman of the board, McCann-Erickson Corporation (International), Mr. Weaver guides the overseas operations in 18 countries with 35 offices. His advertising career started with Young & Rubicam as the producer of the "Fred Allen Show." Later, at the request of George Washington Hill, he joined the American Tobacco Company as advertising manager. In the communications industry he served as president and then board chairman of the National Broadcasting Company. In his introduction, Frank Baker, Conference director, said: "It is difficult to decide whether to introduce Pat Weaver as a creative man with business abilities, or whether he should be described as a creative business man. Obviously, he is both."

13

# the end of "modern times"

I DO WANT to give you the message that, as communicators, we should devote ourselves to distributing around the world, and the method that might be successful. To tell you the message, I must overstate and oversimplify it and get into philosophy.

Frankly, we have reached a new stage in social development with the end of "modern times" and the beginning of our era. This is the last of several stages. The first really started with the American Revolution and with the idea, incredible to men at that time, that men could be equal. This was flying in the entire face of history.

This explosive fact set up the second stage, which was technological. In the course of the second stage, we built a tremendous economy, which brought into perspective a second possibly explosive fact. It was simply that man could look forward to economic equity, and this was an incredible incentive for people.

In this century, we came to the third stage — the acquisition of incontrovertible data of all kinds, on all subjects, at every level. It is a titanic flood of information that has overthrown much, if not most, of what was thought to be true in previous times and in previous fields.

This new information has restructured our universe. It has rebuilt our sciences, accelerated our economy and given us the facts to reassess our total philosophy. The great insights, the information that we now have, have really made us realize without saying it that all previous societies have been founded on information and beliefs that were untrue, inaccurate or, at best, fragmentary.

The fourth stage we are entering — I think we entered it about 1950 because of television — is the communications stage, the "extension, out." That is, of course, if we don't kill each other in the meantime and if we all survive the attacks and heresies against the Western open society. We will go through the communications stage. We'll get the message out, we'll teach the methodology around the world, and then we'll go into a final, glorious stage of modern man in an individualist society. Of course, this will, in terms of human beings and their problems, set up the problems and processes of a new society, which will start new stages, with new problems. But you will be glad to know we won't get into that here. . .

In communications, people who are in the business and who have leadership in the business, should try to get across a basic message. And you have to take the time, if you are in this business, to think, so that you know how much of the message of our times you accept and wherein you want to dissent.

You know, freedom of speech has never meant that all voices have validity. "Equal time for different positions" has nothing to do with "equal merit for different cases," and everybody understands that.

There is a vast area of agreement, for instance, on the general picture that I present. But I would have to admit that there is a terrific, furious opposition to what I think is the message of modern times. You, individually, will have to decide what you think. But it is important, because you are privileged to be in communications and you should straighten out your philosophy. I would hope that a number of you would elect to advance the cause of the individual around the world, and help elevate the condition of the common man to make him the uncommon man.

I know that the stages I've outlined vary in different parts of the world, and we have present "modern times" in many stages. We have absolutism reigning here and there in dictatorships. We don't even have political equality in some places and certainly not technological development. But this is all changing right now with immense rapidity, and if you are in international work, as I am, you can see it happening as you travel.

*15*

### People are basically the same

The demand for freedom we see as one basic, important part of this on a smaller scale, but important to those of us in advertising. The economic change-over around the world from commodities to trademark brands is part of this revolution. Trademark brands are merely a way of guaranteeing a buyer consistency, uniformity and quality. The trademark is an instrument, economically, that has worked very well where it has been used, and it will be used everywhere. It is vitally successful, and it has forced also a distribution pattern somewhat like our own. We are seeing fewer middlemen. We are seeing more of the self-service and supermarket type of distribution and lower cost distribution, around the world.

The use of American advertising techniques world-wide is not going to work without a lot of changes, and I am sure that many Americans will realize that we are bested in our various techniques and audio-visual methods in many places.

In television in Europe, for instance, some of the programming and advertising is fascinating and immensely credible. In poster design and some of the other sales promotion material, what they are doing on the Continent is fabulous.

So that as we get to the problem of our business around the world, I think one thing we do know is that American selling methodology — that is, the use of communications and information in all media and to all people — will work and that our basic economic method, our incentives, will work.

These problem-solving methods are going to be adopted in all societies that have a choice, and we will find that people are basically the same, even though they exhibit differences by community, by region, by country, by area.

Of course, marketing is only part of the total problem I'm particularly talking about. People, however, are the same — whether they buy, vote, hear radio or see television; whether they live in the jungles and hear drums and see witch doctors they are the same people.

The human being, as raw material, is worked upon by the influences of his culture and times, his glands, his opportunities and other factors. While we cannot speak to the German as though he were English, or to the Japanese as though he were an Australian, our basic methodology will work in all places. It will work better if nationals of the countries involved will be in on the actual world image that we are trying to create.

The world is shrinking, the world is booming. You will hear a lot about that in this Conference. We will have to do our work in this perspective in the coming decade.

### The philosophy of leadership

But let me get back to the philosophy of leadership, to the message and the method of communicators. When I called this piece "The End of Modern Times," I did so as an optimist. I am very glad that modern times are over. I have said many times, and I certainly believe it, that the "good old days" were not good. They were bad. The evils in a society in any given time can be excused to the degree where they come from ignorance — like, for instance, human sacrifice, done because of the ignorance of people; and even when they come from necessity, like slavery as a human institution, or a status society as a human institution. When you have not enough for everyone, you have a different solution in terms of social institutions than you do when you have a society of plenty, and this is why there is a guilty feeling among so many intellectuals in our world. It is because we realize that continuing inequities and suffering and misery and inequalities are absolutely unnecessary.

We know enough in this country certainly, right now, to build a society with plenty for all. I believe that with communications dedicated to the proper goals, we will achieve a great acceleration of what we need to solve the problems and to get to that fair day sooner.

Well, let me, if I can, explain why I think we have reached the end of modern times. I am taking as an example what to me is the most shining example of a great country with tremendous contributions. I am referring to Great Britain and the British Empire. They represent a status society, which to an American is difficult to respect because they appear to us to deform their people through their social customs, by the way they operate. But, with their record for democracy, and individualism, and the pattern of beliefs they hold, and the great credit that they are to the human condition, it would be hard not to be great admirers of Britain and the Empire.

Let us look at what they did as they took over countries. They abolished extreme, inhuman customs — suttee in India, for instance. They trained the nationals of the country. They brought in modern medicine and hygiene and they improved transportation. They also developed good, civilized government, among other good things.

What they did, in their belief complex, was to leave the societies they conquered the way they were. This, within their belief complex, was the right thing to do. But, historically, was it not wrong, from the point of view of reference to the new stage that we are in now? And looking backward at modern times, could you not argue that the world would be a better place today if the British Empire and Great Britain, in their various imperial roles, had moved with determination as the communists have done and, throwing out past religious and other forms, replaced them with their own?

By taking the Roman posture, the British felt other nations would follow them by precept and example where appropriate, and England became the steward of these many, many countries around the world. She might, however, have constructed Asian and African societies with fully-educated peoples, parliamentary methods, highly industrialized economies and the other elements of what we call highly industrialized Western society.

It would have been ruthless and, in fact, within the belief complex we have all been raised on in modern times, it would have been impossible. So, when I say she was wrong, I speak from the viewpoint of the next stage of history, and therefore don't really believe it.

I saw the British Empire and, believe me, they did the only thing possible. But I point out to you, within the present amount of knowledge, we can see they did have another choice even though it wasn't really open to them.

No one could ever again set up the kind of leadership over another society and leave that society alone except for perhaps island societies that one wants to leave in their conditions without attempting to modernize them. But no large area could ever be handled that way again. This shows once more the tremendous change that has come over us in our belief complex.

### What is our modern message?

Let's talk about the present, and our problems with the citizens of other colors and others who suffer today from the stigma of status in America and other countries. This is a process, let's face it. We declared that men were equal in 1776, and then forgot them. We went through the Civil War, freed the slaves, and then forgot them. Finally, with the acquisition of knowledge and the opening of our minds, we are realizing that inequity against brothers of any minority group is just simply not tolerable, and we shall do something about it. Before, we worried too much about ourselves, as U. S. people. Since this is an international Conference, I would like to include the rest of the world. We do not have any particular monopoly on injustice. You still have injustice in India, and the slaves in the Arab world. Most of all, you have the impoverished masses of most of the world, who don't know or care what kind of government they work under because they have so little.

The perspective of justice has to be world-wide. None of us are just yet. But the rights of man must be faced up to and must be expedited. The vehicle for this, essentially, is communication.

So, what is our modern message? What does our modern society stand for? Where is it going, and why? As I have said, I believe we are entering a glorious new age. Finally we are washing out the prejudices and fears, and we are eroding away the old customs and habits, usages that have unfairly handled most of mankind in our few thousand years to date.

Our modern message, in my opinion, is very simply a restatement of the individualized, liberal, self-realizing, self-motivated society. It is a problem-solving society, an economy built to make more people creatively effective in producing goods and services through a vast range of incentives. An increasing number of those incentives are being aimed at more than just additional gadgets.

This is an equitable human society that has as its premise the belief that each individual is not only legally as good as

19

the next, but that each individual will have economic equity. This includes healthy surroundings, foods, vitamins, education consistent with the person's ability, opportunity to move into any field in society, to intermingle in any groups in society without feelings of fear or shame or inferiority. And the last point, which is misunderstood by so many intellectuals, is why we must have through our mass communications the elements that will allow people to have uniformity, where differentiation in speech or clothes or habits continue to have any kind of status connotation. "Cockney millionaires" are not the right thing to have.

The day may come when we can go away from uniformity, but not until we have removed "the lower classes." "Lower classes" can be discovered by their accents, or manners, or some other phenomenon of status. As long as that is true, mass media should try to create a wide uniformity at this time among peoples.

Each individual is a center in the economy and as he is challenged so the individual is stimulated. But if it's a welfare state, the individual is protected against the illnesses of our modern times — old age requirements, and so forth. How can we shape our society to protect the individual from things that are beyond his control? How can we nourish in him the appreciation for the finer things that all men in all times have strived for so strongly when they were in the "upper class?" The privileges brought through money or leisure should be available to everyone, because we have the communications to make them available.

How can we relieve people of the tedium and strain of too much work? How can we bring people to maturity so that the whole farce of status drive, tragic as it is, can be replaced with genuine development of talents, the real purpose of self-realization, the exhilarating search for new adventure of the mind and of the spirit?

People keep up with the Joneses simply because they don't know any better. It is entirely a matter of information and communication. Give them the information that we have now, as communicators, and they are going to turn away from keeping up with the Joneses — this vapid effort — to finding real pleasure, real profit, real information in the culture, arts, gardening, travel, sports and a whole range of things.

There are some parts of this process, such as the increasing number of older people who go into leisure with no training, or women who, freed from drudgery by electrical appliances of all kinds, sit mesmerized before television sets much too long, instead of finding out what this leisure can mean to the whole person. And what a world there really is for an average person with leisure, with all of today's instruments and with a little intelligence to use them.

### Man's dreams of a just society

So the message of the future society goes back to those golden dreams of man of a just society with free and equal individuals composing it. There are some violent attacks upon this picture of our society. They come from some enemies but mostly from friends. The liberal tradition is not warmly received by many thinkers any more and the betrayal of our Western philosophy has some imposing names, like Toynbee, Niebuhr, and so on.

I believe that these men all start with a very fundamental flaw: they do not understand that mankind is *child*kind. We have just dropped down out of the trees in terms of real time. True man has not had any social history, just a few broken down societies founded by people who looked upon information that was utterly untrue — in a very brave, and gallant, and admirable way — and tried to do something. We must pity them and admire them, but we must not try to find any information from their experience to guide us in what we can do. It's ridiculous.

There is no past that can give us any indication of our future. Take the communist heresy, as it really should be called by those of us in the West. It denies man's individual worth and dignity, subjects man to an insect-like, collectivist merging, and is based on dogma that is not true. It was revolutionary to Karl Marx, but it's gone.

The capitalist system is not what it was; it is now an incentive system. And the other operations of the communists are getting into a more brutal — immoral, to us — way of making people do things, and paying a tremendous cost in human suffering. So it's something that really means the attraction of the system can only be for those people who feel it is the only one that can work for them.

21

Our past, against these heresies, comes not from evil, not from sin, not from anything but lack of knowledge. Certainty, incidentally, is one of the things we have gotten rid of in modern information techniques; and that gets rid of fanaticism, too, because only men who are convinced are fanatics and today we know enough to know that the sign of a search for certainty is a sign of immaturity.

The Bridgeman insight is the part of proper learning for all communicators, which is simply that we may not ever know with final certainty or final truth. Not because it isn't there to be found out, but because of the way that we as men have been constructed in the course of our evolutionary processes, so that we may never know that final truth. You must accept it and live with it.

### Aim for the superior, not the average

As we grow to adulthood, it is obvious there will be many transitional phases in our lives that are not very good, like status seeking or the need for uniformity for a while. It is said, for instance — and here we have a little more trouble — that in the United States we make a god of the average man. We pressure him to conform at all levels, and we confuse what is excellent with what is average.

I do not happen to believe this. In my experience there is no confusion. The average is supposed to be a marker, and it should always be rising to indicate that people generally are growing in knowledge and intelligence and aiming always for the superior, not the average. The excellent is known for what it is, and it is certainly not average, but we hope that someday it will be average. That is our purpose, to make it average.

But when we have primitives in power in some fields, who are ignorant of the history of our times, ignorant of the needs of man or perhaps not interested in communications in the sense in which I am discussing it, then we have a problem.

Take the motion picture industry for example. I was born in Hollywood. I love movies. Nobody could be happier about movies than I am. Except that they have focused their interests, from a management point of view, on the box office and art. There has never been any concept of audio-visual communications to our people through film presentations, in theatres, that respond to the interests of the people.

Magazines, on the other hand, have built their entire last 25-years' success on non-fiction, on recognizing and serving the broad, basic interests of the American public. These are not in story-telling but in the real world, with some escape and fiction in leisure time efforts, too. But the books such as *Life* and *Look* and *Reader's Digest*, have succeeded because they were not fiction magazines.

Television, during my eight program seasons, made a conscious effort to develop the non-fiction field, the news field and coverage of the real world. Also it was advertising-oriented; that is, the men that I had to deal with were all ad men. They were either clients, or heads of radio and television departments. Therefore, we worked to try to serve the advertising business, because that is how we got the money to do what we wanted to do.

Also, the management in that particular business should be responsible for giving the creative elements new, expanding, horizons in the kinds of things they can create. Writers don't write plays for theatres that do not exist, and it is only when you show people what they can do that they begin to do it.

Well, the facilities, interests of the radio and motion picture industry who together, combined, run the electronics business, do not understand this point of view and have not, to my knowledge, had too much experience with it. The most slipshod of reasons, in communications, is used all too often by men who know better. It is called "giving the people what they want."

You can project, without any question, a degraded series in any field, if you decide that you are going to give the people what they want. I think, in the case of television, the quiz scandals and some possible government action have brought us some better programming. But what we really need are communications officials who realize that "giving the people what they want" is antediluvian in thought.

### Management responsibility

Let me give an example, from television, of what I mean by management responsibility. The spectacular was an event, in one-shot form, that we started in 1954. We had several

23

years of preparation, mainly because the agencies and clients would not let us preempt time. As you know, I have been on all sides of the fence. In fact, I was at CBS before all this. I always moved where the power was going — just seemed like the sensible thing to do — and helped it along.

Most people said the spectacular wouldn't work, that nobody would remember when it was to be on. "You can't change human nature," and so on. This made it very difficult to sell these programs. But we did. By the third season, the agencies and clients got the message, that these tremendous merchandizeables of programming were so great with the trade alone, that even if you forgot to put the show on it would still be worth the money. As professionals, they realized this, and then you had all the other values of exploitation and all the rest.

Result: the form won and, as you know, most of the spectaculars today are run by the agencies and clients, except where they are in time periods where they have to put more in to fill out the time.

But the point is that the form was fought for, and won. It would not have become a part of the business if this had not been done. The people didn't want it because they didn't know what it was. You have problems at any time in business if you do not have the leadership fighting for new things that go against what others may think is true.

Right now, the non-fiction form of programming is in danger because, in the middle of the season, some shows failed. To get credit in Washington or for whatever reasons, suddenly non-fiction starts appearing in the wrong times. Wrongly scheduled, wrongly exploited, the record goes down, and agencies are saying, "You know what that show did? On Saturday night, it got nothing."

Well, this is part of our business. As professionals, we are supposed to know these things. Therefore you endanger the form if you do not fight for it with real professional knowledge all the way through. The public cannot want what it does not know. Management must give the public wonderful things and get the public to understand the wonder of them.

### The power of communication

We need the power of communications to make our people aware of their world and the challenges in it, of the transition into the new society, of the problems ahead, and the alternative solutions. We want to involve the public in these problems, not shield them from them, not reduce them to mesmerized morons by the mass media.

The contrast between the excellence of the profitable enterprise — a great enterprise such as the *New York Times* — and some of the other problems in communications, is alarming. You know, in printed media we have ratings as well, and too many of the printed media follow them. But if the publishers really gave the people what they want (in the electronics pronouncement) our printed material would be the comic strips and the sports pages, nothing else.

So the whole thing is ridiculous and everybody really knows it. Yet last week an important trade magazine said, "The general objective, whether noble or not, is to give the public whatever it wants, and the public can have any fare it wants as long as it wants it badly enough and in sufficient quantities." This was said in a major trade magazine that I will not embarrass by mentioning its name.

All of us know better than this. If we don't, we should get out of the business. We have seen great strides in making people watch what they had never heard of before. For example, I remember the excitement when we got thirty millions to watch "Sleeping Beauty," seven years ago.

There is no question but that these forms are wanted. They must be done right, however, scheduled right and knowledgeably sold. We have to remember that the public will want to be challenged more and more as they grow up, and that we must help them to grow up, not just put them to sleep. Let Hollywood stay in the story-telling field; let them be the merchants of dreams and salesmen of escape. We can use a lot of escape in some directions, but this is not enough.

In radio and television at least, we need the theatre, arena, concert hall and the opera house. The whole point is, the communications' use of television — the concept of serving all interests in the public — influences those interests in terms of information delivered, relaying new adventures that might be offered.

I might remind you that adherence always to quality concepts means immensely profitable quality operations. The drive for quality is the best, the only, basis on which to build a really continuing, growing, prosperous business.

The revolutionary role of communications is understood more easily if you talk of operations. I remember, five years ago, at the National Association of Broadcasters, they outlined and discussed all my programming. This included serious music, opera, ballet, symphony, the regular use of non-fiction, news in depth, and programming in the prime nights. Also the constant, deliberate scheduling of experimental works and innovations of various kinds, all the special programming plans, on top of a drive for regular quality in the regular programming. All this was outlined in forms that included new ways of getting new advertising support in an effective manner, and most of it was talked about as being finally able to be put across by now, 1960.

The thrill and the excitement of this kind of television scheduling and entertainment in non-fiction, in news coverage, in all manner of activities from the symphony to vaudeville, is really tremendous. It can be done by really dedicated, knowledgeable people in all forms of communication.

### Leadership and the fight for quality

We owe it to society to be dedicated to our responsibility. We must fight always for quality. Individually, the method of quality depends on what you do, but hack work and potboiling and "adequate" stuff aren't really enough. Each of us should try to do his job better. We should try to improve, to break through new ground in style, in thought, in technique, in basics of every kind. And those of us who do have this management responsibility must remember that leadership is the key to progress and, in communications, we must forget that primitive, ugly concept of giving the people what they want. Elevate the standard, inspire finer things, enrich those programs that are given to the people under the inspiration of leadership that shows them what can be done. All this will accomplish miracles.

Our leadership in communications throughout all the media must be such that we do inspire our associates to experiment, to be discontented, dissatisfied, to want to change from the first thing that comes along. I know that this can be done. I have been in and out of it and around it, many times. You have to let the people who work under the management know that the different, the new, the experimental, the daring, the bold, will be rewarded — that the way to succeed is to try the harder thing. Men and women will gladly follow the harder path, and writers will find new ways to do non-fiction for higher audiences. They will find stories that reflect credit on the whole race instead of piling brutality and sadism into all the visual art forms.

We should be doing more about the real world, in television, in newspapers, theatres. We should know all the great men of our time intimately, as we started with the "Wisdom" series, many years ago. There are innumerable examples of how a ferment can be created throughout an organization, bringing higher creativity and a finer result from your people, and higher morality and more money for everyone, too.

My point is that leadership can make people far outperform their own basic ability and leadership must be aimed at upgrading the product, increasing its quality, increasing its excitement and bringing, in communications terms, enlightenment as well as escape, upliftment as well as diversion.

There is no excuse for our modern audio-visual communications not to bring us all, across the country and the world, the glory of the theatre, the drama of history, the panorama of our real world and its people and the places in it, and the problems and the alternatives before it.

They are really doing this better in Europe than we are doing here. With the natural liking of the Europeans for this treasury of mankind, the really cultured things, their scheduling in many ways makes ours look quite inferior.

This effort is going to pay off for us, however. The glow which passes to the workers from the leadership, to plan and inspire; the bottom line always reads, bright, black and big: As communicators, you should take the time to understand the times in which you live, and what you think about them. Individually, you have to work for quality of product, for better advertising, for the newer and the finer and the break-through. In leadership roles as you have them or as you obtain them, you must boldly lead to change and to improve. More and more, the world's people realize that we are entering, really, the first adult society, an egalitarian, equitable society — adults, finally.

All previous societies, you can discount. We could learn many things from them. They are thrilling, exciting chapters. But don't try to learn from them what will happen tomorrow. We have more and more people, more and more data, more and more plans and projects that we know can carry us ahead. And we have lots of problems. We need to get going on them very fast, and communications is our method.

I was thinking of such things as intelligent land use, record-ing the entire treasury of mankind audio-visually, so that everyone can see, and hear, and enjoy it. There is no use in having satellites up in the sky relaying more detective and cowboy stories. But, if we can all go to La Scala and the Bolshoi Ballet and take Leonard Bernstein around the world, then we have something.

We must rebuild our educational system, which is not too hard to do again, if you approach audio-visual means with an open mind, and try to do the job instead of merely copying something from your past.

Basically, though, we have great days coming, a great age coming, and in our communications stage that we are enter-ing, the professionals are those on whom much of the re-sponsibility for the future will rest. Be worthy of your roles.

# four families

*a documentary film on family life
in India, France, Japan and Canada*

Written and Produced for the
National Film Board of Canada
by Ian MacNeill

Executive Producer Guy Glover

Commentary by Dr. Margaret Mead

## MARGARET MEAD

Dr. Margaret Mead is Associate Curator of Ethnology, American Museum of Natural History, New York and Adjunct Professor of Anthropology, Columbia University. In her anthropological expeditions, she has lived among primitive races in the South Seas. She is the author of eleven books and the co-author, editor and co-editor of seven others. She is the author and narrator of soundtrack for seven films. She has held 27 lectureships throughout the world and has received many awards. She is at present working on changing conceptions of time and space.

## GUY GLOVER

Born in London, Guy Glover came to Canada as a young child, was educated in Calgary and Vancouver, and graduated with Biology Honours from the University of British Columbia. He has been both an amateur and professional actor and theatre director, as well as writing poetry and literary, film and ballet criticism. Since joining the National Film Board he has collaborated in the production of many short films, and currently, with the Board's television section, he is producing a series of films on Canadian history while continuing the "Comparisons" series.

# four families

Introduction by Guy Glover

**O**N THE BROAD WATERS of communications, among the advanced-design marine craft of one kind or another and among the more decorative swans, documentary film-makers have a barnyard aspect and, like ducks at a regatta, they sometimes have a hard time to up-end themselves and dredge around in the common mud of the river bottom.

The film you are about to see is an example of that kind of dredging, carried out amid the crossed lines, jammed broadcasts, conflicting signals and so on, which seem to beset the headlong rush of contemporary life. The series of hour-long films to which it belongs was devised in order to give us some opportunity to examine our experience in a number of fields of human activities in such a way that we can get a clearer — that is to say, a more objective — view of the kinds of persons we are and of the kind of society in which we live.

We hit upon the idea — I'm sure, by no means an entirely new one — of putting alongside our experience the experiences of other people in parts of the world far removed from our own, and seeing how they and we stack up in the same frame of reference. We might have called the series "Juxtapositions," for our methods in some of these films are little more than that.

But we decided on a more common word for our series, and entitled it "Comparisons." The first film we made of that series was "Four Families." It is an exercise in popular comparative anthropology, dealing with child rearing in four reasonably different cultures. Although the film is entirely conventional in technique, it must be admitted, technically

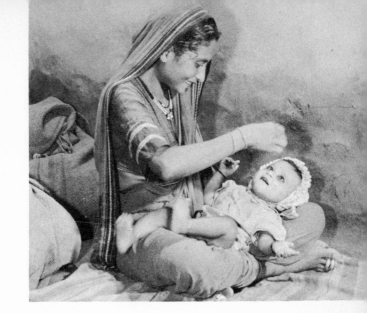

India: the baby wears black beads around his wrist, and a black thread around his waist to protect him against evil.

Japan: The whole family eats together. The baby comes to the table, this time on its mother's back. After the meal the mother gives her baby her breast.

Canada: Instead of the elders performing the religious ceremonies, the mother helps the small boy to take the lead in saying grace.

India: the meal goes on with the father and older children eating together while the mother sits aside feeding the baby milk. She herself will eat alone.

speaking, it is a rough job. The cutting is often merely expedient and the location sound is often shaky and spotty. Part of the reason is that, despite its simple appearance, the material was not simple to record.

Getting unsophisticated people to just be themselves in situations where well-defined work patterns or other activities of an absorbing nature are largely lacking was our director's and cameraman's difficulty. We could not use hidden cameras — the environments and conditions didn't permit it. Our directors had simply to work with the subject long enough and patiently enough and sympathetically enough to create the necessary level of acceptance, and then hope for the best. Some succeeded better than others, but all of them managed to record something real which was therefore something of value for our purposes.

We edited the material and shot the studio framework with Dr. Margaret Mead. Her part in the enterprise was, of course, much greater than that, since she acted as advisor on the whole project and without her advice and collaboration, especially during the planning stages, the film could not have been made at all.

### Discussion

Following the showing of the film, Dr. Mead commented on the concept of "Four Families." Discussion was led by Robert H. Blattner of New York and Colin MacMichael of Montreal.

*Dr. Mead:* This film is the kind of thing that could only be made through a tremendous cooperative effort. I could not possibly get anybody to give me enough money to make a quarter of it. When I want a film for scientific purposes, I have to hide it under the headings of "expendable" or "consumable supplies" — rubber bands, envelopes, film.

There is no support whatsoever in this country for doing scientific films, if you do them just as a scientist. In most parts of our film industry there is not any great enthusiasm for the cooperation of the scientist in making films, either. The unique thing about the Canadian Film Board is that it has always believed in a kind of complex, interdisciplinary tangle in which all kinds of people work together, so that this was an extraordinary opportunity for me to make this film.

*Bath: India*

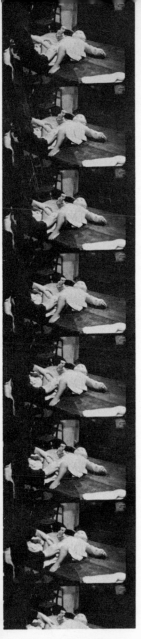

Bath: France

A point that I think should be of interest to all of you, especially those who are trying to work with any kind of overseas group, is that we did not have a detailed script for this. I knew that if they got a bath and a meal and a baby we would have all the material we needed. Even Dr. Aubry in France, with whom I have worked a lot, said she didn't think there would be anything typical enough in the French bit of family life! But you can just trust in culture, and it unrolls before your eyes perfectly satisfactorily.

So all the instructions we had in these films was: get a family, be sure the children are the same age in each country. The most trouble we had was with the Canadian family. At one stage, they wanted to take a family closer to Ottawa and in a more urban setting. This was an important technical point because we didn't want to offend the Indians and the Japanese, but we wanted to have rural and traditional life where there are old costumes and where they did as they once did some time ago. We had to protect their feelings of pride. If we had taken an urban group in North America we would have had to take an urban group there and, in the modern image of Japan and India, you often can't tell the difference between Ottawa and Calcutta.

So the only way to have the kinds of comparisons that the audience would enjoy and that would preserve these traditional differences, was to guarantee that we do something comparable about these other parts of the world. And the only way to do that was to say: everybody will be rural, everybody will be a little bit old-fashioned.

I don't like making a film of this sort without representing at least all three of the great races of Man; but one is limited, again, as to where a film crew is at any given moment. We think that if you keep in mind, in the tone of your voice and in the framing of a particular film the things you want to be doing as well as the things you are doing, you can carry forward an idea, even if you do not have all of the materials before you.

Also, this didn't take very long. At first there was a terrific flurry of activity. We made out the scripts, and sent telegrams because I had to speak to the people around the world who would be the advisors and would locate the villagers. Then, dead silence, until you couldn't believe all this was going on, in France and Japan and India.

33

Suddenly, all the scripts came rushing back, and it was all put together in less than three days' work on my part, because we were working with regularities we knew about and we were working with a network of people who trusted and understood each other, so we could communicate very fast. I only had to write one letter to the experts in the different countries and, because we had worked together in the past, we could tie this together in a short time.

You noticed the Indian was the most critical of her own culture. We had to have her. She had been trained here and had absorbed some of our prejudices. So she is a little bit more critical of her own people, probably, than is quite right objectively. But we thought it was more important to have somebody from each group discussing themselves than to worry about these small details.

*Bath: Japan*

*Mr. Blattner:* From your knowledge of New Guinea and those other cultures which are not in our immediate world, does the same pertain to such things as the love for a baby; the same family conditions that we saw here, do they generally govern?

*Dr. Mead:* Everywhere in the world the babies that survive are treated personally. Just consider what that statement means for a minute. The more simple the people the fewer their resources, the fewer babies they can successfully keep and love and take care of. But also, babies do not survive unless they are treated so that they feel valued by individuals.

When we put babies in orphanages and they are taken care of by paid personnel, they die too; only they die at a distance and we take less notice. So it is possible to go right back to the very simplest people and find this type of constellation of parental responsibility of some kind and the relationship between the way the child is handled and the kind of character it will have when it grows up.

*Mr. MacMichael:* I was very much impressed with one point in the film and that was the quality common in all four families of these children being brought up in a warm nest. I don't mean this in a "coddle" sense, but they all had a sense of belonging in a warm, safe, comfortable place. Was this intentionally planned; were these families picked out especially to present this type of home?

Bath: Canada

*Dr. Mead:* No, our instruction simply was to find a family with a baby and a couple of other children, at about a typical socio-economic level. Now, the Indian was a little too nest-like because in most parts of India you are part of a much more extended family and this again is, I am afraid, the American influence. So that the boundary around that Indian family is not quite correct. To be graphically accurate, there should be perhaps some twenty other people in different parts of the courtyard, at least part of the time.

*Mr. MacMichael:* What I really meant was that there was a different materialistic background in the families. I think the figures were $600 in India, $1,000 in France, $1,600 in Japan for a slightly larger family and, in the Canadian family, we had $9,000 a year. But the washing machines and other evidences of affluence didn't seem to bother the children one little bit, even at that level. It is this warmth of family that seemed to me to come through in all of this. I'm just curious to know if that was part of the actual plan.

*Dr. Mead:* Of course, one would not picture a quarrelsome family, because they wouldn't have been good in the film, and you can just imagine what the filming was like. There was one bit in the French film that we cut out because it was incorrect, untypical—where the children chased each other around the table; they took advantage of the fact of the photographers being there. And in the Japanese family, of course, the photographers had cables laid out in every direction. You had to have good cooperation. So that perhaps the feeling of ease in each family would be a function of the way this was taken.

The willingness to make this kind of film is not something that grew overnight. I remember a Canadian woman broadcaster came down, it must have been eight or ten years ago, and she wanted to find something in common that people had all the way around the world. She started with the idea of vacations and then discovered that in most parts of the world people just didn't have any — which was a blow. She came to see me then and I talked about the fact that the family was universal.

Canada's attitude towards their different immigrant groups, their attempts to respect the cultures of their ethnic groups, all of these things have gone into a climate of opinion that has finally made it possible for the Canadian Film Board to make this kind of film. The importance of building up a whole series of expectations that gradually build up to a new kind of TV or a new kind of communications, that, I think, can't be underestimated. Particularly, in a group like this coming from all over the country and where each person has some kind of a role in building up our attitudes towards other people — in trying to correct, on one hand, our slushy sentimentalities — for example, if we are firmly convinced that others, too, like babies then they are nice people; and if they are not nice people then they are our enemies; but in this way we see something good about them.

There is this need to break down the "all or nothing" picture of an "enemy," which is one of the most pressing things in the world today. We have to recognize the fact that our enemies also like babies; in fact, they are quite good with them and grow them up to be quite good enemies.

Also we must realize that our enemies love peace as much as we do and at the same time we must be able to be vigilant in keeping some kind of an uneasy peace, at least. This is very hard for Americans to do, and this sort of thing helps in working out ways to do it. Now I'm not saying North America either, I'm saying the United States, because I think the Canadians do this more honestly, and this is one of their great contributions.

If we can develop some way of remembering simultaneously that the members of another Society love babies, love their husbands and love their wives, love nature, and want peace, and have loving care in their schools and so forth — and at the same time that their governments are pursuing policies which, unless checked by our Government, may bring a holocaust on the world — this, it seems to me, is one of the most important and necessary tasks facing us. Everyone is building an image of ourselves vis-a-vis the images of other peoples.

# Problems in World Communication

## ASDRUBAL SALSAMENDI

Now information chief of the New York Office of United Nations Educational, Scientific and Cultural Organization (UNESCO), Mr. Salsamendi joined United Nations in 1947 as liaison officer in the Department of Public Information, and served successively as liaison officer in its Paris headquarters and the New York Office of UNESCO. He holds both a B.Sc. and a B.A. from the University of Uruguay. He interrupted his study of law to engage in anti-Nazi activities as director of radio programs of the British Council in Montevideo and head of the Educational Film Department. He was introduced at the Conference by chairman Hawkins as "Uruguay's No. 1 Citizen, a poet, a lecturer and a writer."

37

# problems in world communication

SPEAKING SERIOUSLY about the problems of communications in the world — it's quite an interesting problem. If you go back to 1945 or 1946 for a moment, you will remember, in the United Nations General Assembly, just at the beginning of the whole new era of international organizations, that a resolution was adopted which stated that unless the peoples of the world were well-informed the achievement of peace, which is the main task of the UN, would not be possible.

I do believe that that was the first time in which the problem of information was focused at the proper angle. If the UN wants to achieve peace, they need to have the peoples of the world well-informed, and we shall come back to that point later.

In this enormous family of international organizations is UNESCO — and I am delighted to have been introduced in the proper way, by the reference to United Nations Educational, Scientific and Cultural Organization. Recently, I was introduced as representing the United Educational, Social and Cultural Organization. A few years ago, I was introduced to a very high government official and that gentleman said, "I am very pleased to meet someone who belongs to that tiny, wonderful country which so gallantly fought the Nazis in the last war." I have also heard that UNESCO was a Rumanian lady in exile.

As you can easily imagine, from my own line of work, it is quite destructive to have to feel that, in different areas of the world, UNESCO could be a Rumanian lady in exile or a very gallant country, when it is simply an international organization involved with one very simple task—simple to define and very difficult to achieve—which is *to obtain lasting peace through education, science, culture and mass communications.*

I have mentioned that unless the peoples of the world are well-informed it is not possible to achieve peace. In the Constitution of UNESCO there are two sentences, which are for me and possibly for you, very interesting. One says, "Since wars begin in the minds of men, it is in the minds of men that the defenses of peace must be constructed." There is also another sentence in the Constitution of UNESCO which says, "We shall use all of our media, all our ways to use all of our media of communication to the world, to make the world know what we are doing."

### What do we know about UNESCO?

Now that I have mentioned "mass communications," I believe that we are in quite an interesting position. We are in a very highly developed country — the United States — not only economically, and not only scientifically and culturally and socially, but in mass communications as well. If you take into consideration our own criteria, to find out what is a developed country, or an underdeveloped country, or an underdeveloped country in mass media, you would be surprised. Our criteria state that a country is not developed in mass communications when there are less than ten newspapers, less than five radio sets, and less than two theatre seats per 100 persons. In the United States, we have more, much more, than ten newspapers per 100 persons, much more than five sets of radios per 100 persons, and much more than two seats in a theatre per 100 persons and, I wonder, do the Americans know about UNESCO?

This is a very interesting question and it is a challenging problem for me. You could have, in countries which need an international organization, a much more devoted and constant interest, and that is natural. For instance, in India, UNESCO is far better known than here, for the reason that many of our projects have been directed, in fact, to the development of India.

Is the American public informed about UNESCO, and if not, why not?

39

A group of villagers in Delhi State, India, listening to a radio broadcast on a loudspeaker provided by Norway through the UNESCO Gift Coupons program.          UNESCO PHOTO

### What should people be informed about?

Then we come to another very interesting problem, a fascinating problem: What are the things that people should be informed about? You have the media, you have the physical material to work with. But there are millions of items of news, in every country, every minute; millions of news items in New York, particularly, as a nerve center in all these international organizations of the world.

Now, when the selection of news is made, and when a fact is transmitted to the public, in that moment what we call "news" is not news any longer, it is something much more important. It is an element, which is going to belong to the people, which is going to influence the people. Any one of them can have a tremendous psychological impact, and people in the advertising world know this better than me. You change the thoughts of people, you create needs, you create a need to have two television sets, for instance. You can do that. You can create the need to have two cars. You can create the need to have one suit, or two or three per season. These are wonderful things, if you can afford them.

*Children reading books from the mobile library van in the village of Bowana, India.*                    UNESCO PHOTO

On the other hand, that "news" is not only creating one particular idea in the mind of one person, but also it is going to create attitudes from country to country. In other words, "news" can be the means of shaping the world of tomorrow.

It is very timely, I think, that we should be discussing these problems of communications in the world, when 80 per cent of the population of the world has not the facilities to know what is going on in the world. In Southeast Asia, there are extensive regions in which there is not one single newspaper and, of course, there are no radio sets. Then, how can we build the defenses of peace if we cannot communicate with the peoples?

UNESCO is working very hard in trying to develop mass media activities in the different regions of the world. As an example of our work may I say that we called the first meeting in Bangkok in 1960, for Southeast Asia. A great number of problems were discussed, from how to get manufacturers to produce cheaply for very low income people to the price of each word sent by cable from one country to another. As there are many other problems I won't attempt to bore you with details. I am just trying to give you some information for you to think about. The problem is how we can communicate to each other, even if we have the facilities and even if we know that people can reach us, in whatever language we can use.

### How can we communicate to each other?

In the world today there is a very sad picture of this particular subject. Around 46 per cent of the adult population of the world today is illiterate. And around 250-millions of children today do not have facilities to study; they will not have any education at all in their lives, unless the conditions in our world change radically.

What UNESCO is doing to solve that problem, as well as to solve other problems in the fields of science and culture, and in making the people know a little bit better, from one area to another, is just to act as a sort of catalytic element, just to try to force the attention of the different governments in each of the areas of the world, on the same problems and to get their reactions for defining the general principles.

When the principles are adopted, for instance, "free compulsory and universal primary education," then we can go into the planning, taking into consideration the situations of different countries, and being very realistic — because it's all very nice to see plans on paper, but it's quite frustrating not to be able to implement them.

*A primary school in France.*
UNESCO PHOTO

You cannot accomplish those plans unless you are completely realistic. But that does not mean we do not have the space to dream. We dream and try to break through this enormous, vicious circle of ignorance and lack of understanding, just as soon as we can and wherever we can.

### Declaration on freedom of information

I said, earlier, that this was a very timely moment to consider problems of communications, because the Social Committee of the Economic and Social Council of the UN has been discussing the draft of a Declaration on Freedom of Information, which would precede a Convention on Freedom of Information. In this discussion, you could see very clearly how people can scarcely understand each other unless con-

An evening at the Télé-club, Aisne, France. This
was an agriculture program on television organized by
UNESCO and Radiodiffusion Télévision Francaise.
UNESCO PHOTO

Illiteracy in Calabria, Italy.
UNESCO PHOTO BY DAVID SEYMOUR

cessions can be made; fortunately concessions are being made on the two main sides of this problem.

I was fascinated in hearing the debates of the Committee, which has the advantage of having a great number of outstanding representatives. On the one side, the majority considered that the main thing for freedom of information is to let the people say whatever they wish; in other words, including communications which are wrong. On the other side, it was said that you can send communications which are right, but that their effect may be wrong. For example, in reporting how many rapes have occurred in a particular society, the communication in itself is right, but the idea that you may form of that particular society may be wrong because of the emphasis. For that reason, some countries are pressing another point, which is also very interesting: that communications should be accurate and non-distorted, and directed so as to favor friendly relations among countries.

We know pretty well that the Declaration on Freedom of Information is nothing more than a paper. But sometimes papers are much more explosive than bombs. For instance, there is a paper called the Universal Declaration of Human Rights. This was proclaimed by the United Nations on the 10th of December, 1948. From that time till now, that little paper has produced more extraordinary consequences than even the most optimistic members of the UN have ever thought about. And it is used, widely used, around the world, when the rights of people are disregarded.

What we are planning to do in the problem of communications of today is, first of all, to train personnel in the different areas. In Strasbourg, France, we have established an Institute of Higher Studies of Journalism. We established another one in Quito, Ecuador, last year. We are going to establish an Institute of Graphic Arts in Calcutta, India, in which we are going to teach and we are going to train, from the most elemental problems in journalism to the most complicated — in printing, in the organization of a newspaper, in visual material, in research and everything that is connected with it.

We have already organized a Conference, as I mentioned, in Bangkok, in Southeast Asia, to study all the problems of mass communication in the area. We are going to call, in 1961, another similar Conference in Santiago, Chile, and in 1962 there will be another similar Conference in Addis Ababa, Ethiopia, for Africa.

The idea of these conferences is first of all to know what the conditions of today are in each region, and how those conditions can be improved to allow all the people to exercise that social right of being well informed in which we are so interested.

It is possible to accomplish that right only in countries which have facilities, or where they are interested in that particular problem. In some cases, the facilities are such that there is the risk of not reporting about many things because there is too much "news." This is another of the problems that we face.

I would like very much to have advice on how to make the American public know what UNESCO is, and destroy the idea that it is a Rumanian lady, or a small and gallant country.

I hope that my message is simple. First of all, that UNESCO exists; second, that it is a useful organization; third, that we are trying to achieve peace through education, science, culture, and mass communications; fourth, that the situation in the world, because of lack of communications, is deplorable — as it is in the educational field, as it is in many ways in the scientific fields, and as it is in many more ways in the cultural field.

But we are working, and we are working hard. We have had the good fortune to obtain help from all of the countries of the world, from people who know, who believe in our kind of crusade, who believe that the world could be saved, and that it is possible that in the minds of men the defenses of peace can be constructed.

**Questions and Answers**

*Mr. Philip Goyert of Cincinnati:* How much do international politics and bungling diplomacy, in some cases, interfere with the activities of UNESCO?

*Mr. Salsamendi:* In this particular area, UNESCO and the subjects that we are discussing are not quite so much involved with international politics. Our practice is to meet with the governments of the states of one region and try to solve the problems which are utterly essential for these countries.

The importance of the problems make it vital that a quick solution be reached, and our ideas seem to be gaining ground. For example, recently, I heard for the first time the Director of the International Bank for Reconstruction and Development make the statement in the UN Economic and Social Council that the first investment and the most important for economic development is the one dedicated to education.

We have been fighting for that idea for years but, apparently, people seemed to think that education was perhaps a luxury. If you look at the picture of the world today, the countries which are most backward are those which have the highest rate of illiteracy and in which the workers have very little education.* Consequently the problem of politics is hardly a major one in UNESCO.

*Mr. Leroy Winbush of Chicago:* Does UNESCO have any type of exhibit which could be shown in libraries, schools and various places in the United States so that the United States might be informed first, and then circulated in other countries?

*Mr. Salsamendi:* In every member country there is a National Commission for UNESCO. The United States has such a Commission, but with a reduced budget it becomes difficult to inform the people about UNESCO. The materials we have are few. We always have to trust that the organizations within the different countries will reproduce them and show them to the people of each country.

One publication which I would strongly recommend to any one of you who is interested in knowing about UNESCO ideals is *The UNESCO Courier*. It is an exceedingly good magazine, very well printed. Unfortunately there are only 7,000 subscribers in the United States despite the fact that its price is $3.00 a year. Our sales agent, The UNESCO Publication Centre, is located at 801 Third Avenue, New York City, where you can find all our material.

* See "Symbology vs. Illiteracy" by Dr. Frank C. Laubach in *Symbology: The Use of Symbols in Visual Communication*, Edited by Elwood Whitney for the Art Directors Club of New York (Hastings House, 1960).

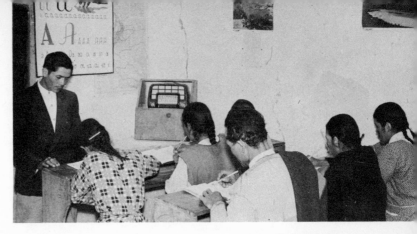

*An unseen voice teaches in the radio school in Satatanza, Colombia. This is a test school operated by members of UNESCO's technical assistance team in Colombia to determine the effectiveness of posters as a teaching device.* UNESCO PHOTO

Returning to the question of exhibits, we do have some exhibits—a magnificent exhibit about Human Rights, another, an exhibit of reproductions of masterpieces of painting, and a third a collection of Persian miniatures. However, we cannot distribute them because it is too expensive and we do not have any budget for traveling exhibits around the world. We do have filmstrips and slides. In mass communication, we have quite a number of publications. Among them are:

*Professional Associations in the Mass Media: Handbook of Press, Film, Radio, Television Organizations*
*World Communications (3rd revised edition)*
*Broadcasting Without Barriers*
    by George A. Codding, Jr.
*The Training of Journalists*
*Paper for Printing Today and Tomorrow*
    by the Intelligence Unit of *The Economist* (London)
*Television and Rural Adult Education*
    by Joffre Dumazedier
*The Entertainment Film for Juvenile Audiences*
    by Henri Storck

Mr. Winbush: Exhibits seem to me the fastest and easiest way to communicate with a number of people. Isn't there a government agency that would be able to appropriate the amount for the budget that would be needed?

Mr. Salsamendi: This is the responsibility of the National Commission of UNESCO in the United States. The National Commission is a body of 100 persons who are appointed by the President and by the Secretary of State. It has an exceedingly small Secretariat, and its appropriation is not large.

47

*Mr. Goyert:* Here we are in a country with probably the greatest system of mass communications that there is, and yet we know so little about UNESCO. Where does this fault lie? It can't be the fault of our media or the receptiveness of our people, I'm sure.

*Mr. Salsamendi:* I will try to be as honest as I can in answering this question, as I always try to be, which usually is a very undiplomatic attitude. I do not believe that this is the fault of the United States essentially. It is one of those things that happens when you have a society that is exceedingly specialized and grown up.

To give you an example, last December I went on home leave. I went to see an editor of a newspaper and asked him to publicize *The Courier.* The next morning, practically half a page of that daily newspaper contained an article about *The Courier,* just because I was his friend.

Now, I cannot go up to the *New York Times* and say, "Look, because we're friends, why don't you publish this?" I can't ask them to publish half a page. If I did, it might land me in Bellevue.

As you can see, it's not the fault of the United States; it's not the fault of the mass media, it's the type of society in which we are living.

My problem is how to sell UNESCO and its spokesman, *The Courier.* For the moment I am doing it to groups like this one, person to person. I'm finally just coming back to what is probably a pre-historic system of mass communication — just talking — which is, I think, the only way that I have at the moment.

*Mr. Winbush:* What about the various school systems as a means of information about UNESCO? If we started with the school systems, wouldn't this thing go on and on and grow into the thing that you would like to see?

*Mr. Salsamendi:* We are in contact with the National Education Association and we have been in contact with all of the organizations connected with that. We are working and we are trying, through the libraries and the schools, and working and trying with the student unions, but we are moving very slowly.

# Peace Through Understanding:
# The 1964 World's Fair in New York

## DOUGLAS LEIGH

A director of the New York World's Fair Corporation and president of Douglas Leigh, Inc., Mr. Leigh was introduced by Frank Baker as "a Southern boy, with imaginative and big ideas, who during the height of the depression, with a capitalization of $150, formed the firm that bears his name. Since then, he has conceived, constructed and lighted to dazzlement, some of the most spectacular 'spectaculars' ever known." The officially stated definition of his firm as an agency which "specializes in over-sized advertising display using neon or lamps in unusual animations" is a triumph of understatement. Leigh's soaring imagination has resulted in 39 "spectaculars"—steaming coffee cups, men blowing smoke rings, giant soap bubbles, waterfalls on Broadway to mention a few. Now he is turning his inventive genius to a new form of communication—The New York World's Fair.

# peace through understanding: the 1964 world's fair in new york

**T**HE WORD "FAIR" is so much a part of our language that it immediately evokes a series of mental pictures. In different languages, the word differs — "fiesta," "feria" or, as we know, "fair" — but the connotation is still the same. The picture does not change, for the fair is a creation of man and traces his beginnings to time immemorial. Its uses have been of varying character.

In medieval times, the fair was used by farmers to barter the fruits of the earth and their labors for necessities which they, themselves, could not produce. The basic character of the fair and the products it displays or sells have always been a reflection of the people. The Fair has become a symbol of man's desire to display his abilities, his wares, his hopes, his creations and his dreams of the future to his fellow men.

Possibly the earliest recorded mention of a fair comes from the Book of Esther in the Old Testament, which describes how King A-Hazurus assembled the rulers and Princes of Persia and Medea to show them the riches of his excellent majesty. It is recorded that this exposition lasted for 180 days, which by coincidence is about the length of most world's fairs today.

Man is still attempting to display his majesty. But today we have found a majesty in ideals and in ideas, and it is in the furthermost of these ideas that modern man has adopted the age-old technique of the fair.

What may be considered the modern world's first exposition took place in Hyde Park in London in 1851 — 110 years ago. There still stands in Hyde Park the architectural symbol of

Trylon and Perisphere, outstanding architectural symbol of the 1939 New York World's Fair.

WORLD WIDE PHOTOS

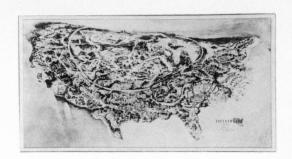

Artist's conception of Freedomland, said to be the largest family amusement center in the world.

United States Pavilion at 1958 World's Fair in Brussels.

Biblical tapestry of King A-Hazurus displaying the wealth of his kingdom in what well may have been the world's first recorded fair.

Rocket attraction at Disneyland, internationally famous amusement center.

Main Street, Disneyland.

this first London Exposition — the Crystal Palace. This edifice was imitated in America two years later, in 1853, and erected in New York in Bryant Park.

There followed in rapid succession for the remainder of the 19th Century a considerable number of fairs and expositions. One of the most notable of these was the Paris World's Fair of 1889. Its crowning achievement, of course, was the Eiffel Tower. The wonder of its age, The Eiffel Tower has become the tangible symbol of France to all.

During the last half of the 19th Century, World's Fairs were as frequent as are westerns on television today. Cities, industries, organizations, anyone could seize upon the flimsiest pretense, throw up a tent, raise a flag, beat the drums and say, "Come to our World's Fair."

This gave rise to the creation of an international organization to authorize and control World's Fairs. This organization is called the "Bureau of International Expositions," better known by officials everywhere as BIE.

The great World's Fair at New York in 1939 offered the theme, "The World of Tomorrow," but failed to presage the horrors that lay immediately before the world. However, many things then shown and predicted for the future have since come to pass, such as color television, jet propulsion, air conditioning, automation, and so on.

There are of course many kinds of fairs — exhibitions and expositions, agricultural or trade fairs, state and country fairs, etc. But the true world's fair — as for example the recent 1958 Fair in Brussels — embraces all. It exhibits the products and accomplishments of the past and present, and offers glimpses into the future.

A recent and unique contribution to the history of entertainment expositions is Disneyland. This exhibition is four-fold in its theme: embodying Frontierland, which pays tribute to Pioneer America; Fantasy-Land, which dwells in the imagination of the young; Adventure-Land, which is a tribute to the Spirit of Man; and Tomorrow-Land, which offers a glimpse into the future.

Another new vehicle for the communication of ideas is the exhibit, recently opened right here in New York, known as

Freedomland, U.S.A. It's the American Story brought alive. It's a telescope back through time, a rollicking fun trip through our nation's past, with a bow to the future at Cape Canaveral.

Located on a 205-acre tract in the Bronx, it is a multi-million-dollar outdoor family entertainment center, where visitors can see not only our history but become a part of it. Appropriately, it has been built in the contour of the map of the United States.

Perhaps the greatest exposition ever will be the coming 1964 New York World's Fair. The event it commemorates — the tercentenary of New York City — is itself an illustration of how far we have traveled in international relations in the last 300 years.

Mutual knowledge and trust are the goals which dictate the theme of the New York World's Fair of 1964, "Peace Through Understanding." The Fair will be a vast gathering where the peoples of the world will show who they are, how they live, what they do and what new heights they hope to reach for the lasting betterment of mankind.

The 1964 World's Fair can only serve to underscore the basic similarities between all peoples, despite the differences in race, languages, and cultures. They will help us know each other better. They will help make it easier for us to live together in "Peace Through Understanding."

New York is a World Center. From the top of the United Nations Headquarters, it will be possible to look directly at the New York World's Fair of 1964, only a few short miles away.

Many of the halls and the buildings of the New York World's Fair of 1964 will rest on foundations of steel and concrete. The Fair, itself, will rest on a more solid, though less tangible support. It will rest on the spirit, the mind, the ability and the resources of men who are dedicated to the creation of a fair, the form and appeal of which is worthy of its noble theme.

The success of the New York World's Fair of 1939 was due in no small measure to the wholehearted support of some of the ablest citizens in this city and country. The New York

Hall of Science and Carillon Tower of World's Columbian Exposition in Chicago, 1893.

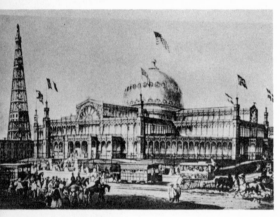

Crystal Palace constructed in Bryant Park, New York to house America's first world's fair in 1853. Named after the original Crystal Palace of the 1851 London Exposition, New York's structure was destroyed by fire in 1856.

MUSEUM OF THE CITY OF NEW YORK

Eiffel Tower, famed landmark constructed at the Paris World's Fair in 1889.

## Peace through Understanding: the 1964 World's Fair in New York

World's Fair of 1964 is similarly fortunate. From its earliest beginnings, this great project was enthusiastically embraced by representatives of every facet of community life, business and education and science, industry, labor and the arts. The roll call of its supporters — and their numbers are growing every day — reveals a long list of distinguished figures.

These are men who call New York home. They are leaders of industry and commerce, who call New York their headquarters. But it is more than mere civic pride that impels them to promote and work for the World's Fair of 1964 in New York; rather, it is because they are world-minded citizens, who realize that the great potential of a World's Fair with so inspiring a theme can be most fully attained in the world center that is New York.

They recall the miracles of science and industry that were exhibited in 1939, for the "World of Tomorrow." We now see them as commonplace services and products, a brief 20 years later. They dare to hope that the New York World's Fair of 1964 will leave an even greater inheritance to mankind, in a much more vital area; it is almost axiomatic to say that what you see in any major fair is a preview of science, industry and architecture of the future.

The site at Flushing Meadows, comprising 1,257 acres, is all ready for the planners, the architects and the artisans, who will make this great dream a reality. In 1939, 63 foreign governments and international bodies, 31 American States, scores of individual corporations and business associations found ample room to display their wares, tell their stories, and make their promises for the World of Tomorrow. 45-millions of people, an impressive new record for fair attendance, passed their turnstiles and more than three-quarters of a million people attended the Fair on a single day.

The increased interest in world fairs, the improved facilities for travel, the greater leisure enjoyed by more peoples, will assure a much greater attendance in 1964. It is not inconceivable to expect an attendance of 70- to 80-millions of visitors to New York's next World's Fair.

Close to 200,000 visitors can be brought to the Fair by subways, trains, buses, automobiles, and even helicopters. That is accessibility. They will come from every one of the fifty

States of the Union and from every country of the world. They will come by the millions from "across the street," from New York City and vicinity. The Host City will contribute the largest number of visitors to the Fair, because Metropolitan New York has a 15-million population to draw from.

The site, the record, the planning and the facilities promise that the New York World's Fair of 1964 will be the brightest landmark in international exposition history.

The theme of the Fair, "Peace Through Understanding," and the universal support it is winning, promise to make it an encouraging landmark in man's relation to his fellow man, a dynamic force in man's constantly improving relations with his fellow man.

# Am I a Camera?

## PHILIPPE HALSMAN

Having first established his reputation as a photographer in Paris, Mr. Halsman escaped the Nazi invasion and came to this country on an emergency visa through the intervention of Albert Einstein, and since 1940 has made New York his home. He is reputed to hold the world's record for *Life* covers, being credited with at least 86. He is the author of several books, the most recent one being a candid study of the great and near-great entitled "Jumpology," the expression of a private theory of Mr. Halsman's that character can be best delineated by the act of jumping. In his introduction, Mr. Baker defined Mr. Halsman as "a sensitive man, with a great ability to create, a marvelous capacity to think clearly, an imaginative wit, and a man who is extremely articulate."

# am I a camera?*

A FEW YEARS AGO, I was asked to photograph Prime Minister Churchill in his home. I thought it would be a good idea to begin by interviewing his secretary and his son, Randolph, for background. Randy said, "Don't start by shooting the Old Man immediately for the final portrait. Shoot him first in the garden and, if you can get him to go out there, he'll show you his goldfish, and then the pigs and, gradually, he'll begin to warm up to you."

My wife and I arrived at about lunch time. We went through a long hall, where Churchill keeps his canvases stacked. He had many hundreds of them, 1,400 or 1,600. And suddenly I realized that the second World War was really nothing more than a contest between two very mediocre and amateurish painters. Only those who know what it is to be an unsuccessful painter can understand the hatred that such a conflict can produce.

When I photographed Mountbatten and Macmillan they had invited my wife and me for lunch. But not Churchill. He finished his lunch and went to his study. I immediately said, "Would you like to go for a walk in the garden, Mr. Prime Minister?" and Churchill answered, "Why? Do I look so bloated?"

He sat down at his desk, and immediately I took a photograph. Churchill said, "You've taken a picture!." I said, "Yes, shouldn't I, Mr. Prime Minister?" He said, "You should warn me." So I said, "All right, Mr. Prime Minister, I'm warning you now, I'm going to take another one." He said, "Not like that. Count." I said, "Count: one, two, three?"

* Photographs copyrighted by Philippe Halsman.

Winston Churchill.

Dr. Albert Einstein.

He said, "No, three, two, one," and then like a bombardier releasing a bomb I was counting, "Three, two, one" and shooting. At one point Churchill had a very interesting expression, and I decided to sneak one in, but he growled at me, "You didn't count." And so I continued counting. Then he interrupted me and said, "Would you like me to make a benevolent expression?" I said, "Please, sir," and he said, "Count!" I counted, "Three, two, one." Churchill smiled, and I got a benevolent expression.

I dont want to bother you with all the details of the sitting. Eventually, he felt some friendship towards me and when I left he gave me a cigar, not one that he had smoked but a fresh cigar. And, since I don't smoke, I gave it to my dentist who appreciated it.

But the great surprise was that there was a picture and this picture was published as a *Life* cover and also on the jacket of Churchill's *Memoirs*. This is obviously one of the greatest men I ever photographed. It's a great face, but you see already the beginning of the fall and decline of the great face.

The other great man, who was in the same class, was Professor Einstein. I talked with him about the atomic bomb. He felt terribly guilty about it, because he felt he was responsible, through his famous formula: $E=mc^2$, through his intervention with President Roosevelt, and some of this sadness is instilled here.

**Photographing women**

Then, I've photographed also women. One of the women that I've photographed, just at the beginning of her career, is this girl, Brigitte Bardot. I went to Paris. She was just married and when I was there in her little room I was scared, because everything in her was pointing at me. Later, I brought the pictures to *Life* and said, "This could be the greatest sex queen of them all," but they filed these pictures away. Later, she became exactly what I said.

But sometimes you photograph a girl and then the very picture that you take suddenly changes her life. For instance, once I photographed an absolutely unknown girl, eighteen. Her name was Ricki Soma. Her father is a restaurant owner,

Bardot—"Everything in her was pointing at me—I was scared."

and this photograph made her suddenly come to Hollywood, and she is now Mrs. John Huston.

Another girl I discovered, at 15, when she was very poor, was France Nuyen. Then *Life* Magazine sent me around the world, to 16 different countries to photograph the most beautiful girls, and did I hate that! Also, these pictures changed their lives.

For example, a Japanese girl became, after her picture appeared, a famous personality, "the most beautiful girl in Japan," recognized by America, and she also became very successful as a model. Another was an Israeli girl, Nurith Pilzer. A young American man saw this picture, fell in love with her and went to Israel to marry her. Then, the Swedish girl, Anita Edberg (not Eckberg), became a television personality. And finally, an Italian girl, but, since I might tell a little story about her that is slightly off color, I'll not mention her name.

I was in Rome and I had to find a beautiful girl and it was almost impossible. The people said, "Well, it's summer now. You should go to Capri or Venice, and so on." But I went to a photographer and said, "Will you show me all the beautiful girls that you have photographed lately?" There was a girl who caught my eye. I went to see her. She was, at that time, 17, and was living with her mother. She was dressed all up for me in the only American dress she had.

I told her, "I want to photograph you as an Italian beauty, so do you have something Italian to wear?" The only thing she had was a red skirt and a green blouse. I said, "Fine. Just go and change into that."

I forgot to tell you, I was accompanied by a researcher, a young man. We waited for five, ten, fifteen minutes and she still didn't come out of the bedroom. I went and knocked at the door. The mother said to come in. When I came in, there was the mother with her daughter, and the girl had not a stitch on and was holding a dress in front of herself. So I pretended I didn't see her and I said, "I have very little time. How long will it take her to change the dress?" and the mother said, "Just one minute." Then she looked at her daughter and said, "Rosanna, you're covering yourself! Don't you see the signor is an artist?" The poor daughter blushed and said, "Mama, I'm ashamed." The mother said, "You're ashamed? I'm ashamed! What kind of a daughter did I bring up, who is ashamed in front of an artist?"

So the daughter put her dress down and I saw the most glorious figure. I tapped the mother on the shoulder and said, "You have done a wonderful job, Signora," and both women beamed. I went out and saw my poor researcher waiting in the living room. I took him by the hand, knocked at the door again and said, "Signora, he is also an artist."

This girl has now become the No. 3 movie actress in Italy, No. 3 after Lollobrigida and Loren.

### Photography has limitations

From the outside all of this looks very glamorous: meeting the most important men, the most beautiful women of our age, sometimes being able to change a life with a photograph. Well, with some photographers, this might lead to a swelled head. In my case, I spend so many hours in the dark room, it only leads to swollen feet. And even more frustrated than my feet is my soul. I feel photography as a means of communication has too many limitations. Here, I would like to introduce you to my thinking, or thinking which is my own.

Man started with one medium of communication — the visual one. He drew on the walls of caverns and caves, and the Egyptians made the first picture stories with their hieroglyphics. Then, probably, the Phoenicians invented the alphabet. This was the second medium of communication, which I call the acoustic one, because although we read with our eyes, the nature of script is actually acoustic. It is nothing but a transcription of sounds, and a blind person using Braille can read the script aloud.

For more than 2,000 years our civilization was carried, disseminated and dominated by this acoustic medium. Writers and orators became the leaders of the modern world. Acoustic strongmen, like Mussolini and Hitler, came into power because they knew how to use the acoustic medium directly or through radio. Even we in the United States select, every four years, our Presidents, after a tremendous acoustic battle.

But suddenly the old, abandoned visual method of communication took its revenge. With the invention of photography, the medium exploded into a force of tremendous power. Within 100 years, this force achieved what it took the written word 3,000 years to do. Let us compare the two media.

In the beginning, only the initiated, usually the priests, knew the secret of writing. Similarly, in the first decades of photography only a few experts could take photographs. After this period came the time of the public scribe, who made his living by writing for people who could not write; and similarly, in photography, there were commercial photographers, who made their living taking pictures for others. Finally, there came the time when practically everybody could read and write, and now we live in an era when practically everybody can photograph. Statistics show there are 70-millions of cameras in the United States in use. We are surrounded by the picture medium: posters, pictures in newspapers, movies, comics, television. It's so bad that the teachers complain the children don't want to read, they only want to look at pictures!

Yes, the visual medium has more appeal than the acoustic one. It has also a much greater impact. I remember when the public read about Hitler's concentration camps. It was appalling, but when the pictures were published, we really got it right in the pits of our stomachs.

But in one respect the visual medium is tragically limited. It cannot express ideas. It can only express everything that is concrete and that can be seen. You can translate the following sentence, word by word, into a photograph: "In a clean, modern kitchen with baby blue walls, a beautiful blonde girl in a red house dress was smilingly peeling a banana." Acoustically, it sounds unattractive. But visually it might be very suggestive.

But how can you express visually this sentence: "The growth of an idea is often stymied?" You cannot show visually a single word of this sentence. In the first sentence, you could show each one of the words, but here you cannot show "growth," nor "idea," nor "often," nor "stymied." This is the limitation of our visual medium: it can show facts, but it cannot express ideas. In my free time, consciously or unconsciously, my endeavor as a photographer became the attempt to push these limits further.

### Expressing abstract figures visually

I'll show you some of my attempts to express visually more or less abstract ideas. But here I would like to make a parenthesis: Please don't think that I try to appear as a great pioneer and trail blazer. We, I mean you and I, are working in a very young and a very unique area. There is probably no one who, from time to time, has not tried to make a picture, or to use a picture, in a way it has not been used before.

All I want to do now is to show a few of my modest examples. The first example is this. One day I read in Dali's autobiography that Dali remembered his prenatal life. He described his recollection of his life in the womb of Mrs. Dali, Senior, in detail.

I decided that I wanted to make a picture to translate this idea, and I came to Dali. This was, by the way, the first time that I met him. I explained my idea: I wanted to photograph him curled up as an embryo and superimpose this in an egg.

Dali said, "It's a sublime idea, but for this picture I have to be naked." I said, "Of course. Will you please take off your clothes?" Dali said, "No, not today. Next Sunday." So, the next Sunday I came over and made the picture of Dali, ready to spring into life.

By the way, he couldn't bring his knees close enough to his chin. I told him, "Well, all right, put your hands around your knees and bring them closer to your chin." He said, "No, no, an embryo never holds his hands around his knees." So suddenly I realized, he really did remember.

Now, another example. An article in *Life* Magazine explained that here in America the men are getting more feminine and women are becoming more masculine and that, eventually, the two sexes will move closer to each other and become indistinguishable. I made a picture to express this idea.

Then, about half a year ago, *Life* ran a cover story on Zsa Zsa Gabor and her ghost writer, Gerold Frank; I wanted to show that the man was a ghost writer, and so I simply photo-

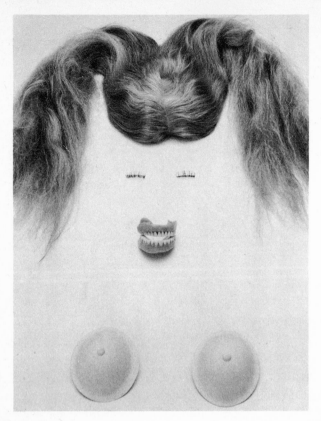

*The Essence of Glamour.*

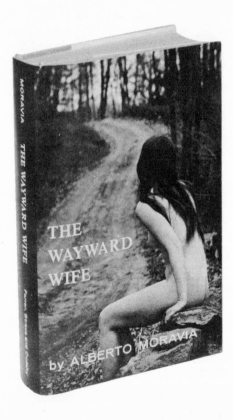

*The New York Times censored her torso.*

graphed him behind a semi-transparent curtain, which made him look like a ghost.

Once *Ladies' Home Journal* asked me to illustrate the idea that it is very unhealthful for sick people to spend all their time in bed because the lying, alone, makes you weak; not the disease, but just lying in bed might kill you. So I made a picture, and I'll not tell you all the trouble I went to, and how I was afraid for my reputation, to be surprised with a skeleton in bed.

Another picture happened this way: I photographed a Holly-wood actress, who had better remain nameless. She brought false eyelashes, false hair, and the rubber things you see un-derneath, and I suddenly decided to make an abstraction. I put also some false teeth in it, and called it "Hollywood Glamour." My brother-in-law, who is French, said, "You know, after all, she's not so bad."

Once, for an advertising picture, I had to photograph a knight's armor, and as my mind always turns in the same circles, I called it, "Where is the can opener?"

A year ago, I had to photograph a jacket of the book, called *Two Women*. The publisher described to me what was in this book, and I make this jacket. People told me, "How come you captured the entire essence of the book in one picture?" I said, "It was very simple, I didn't read it." As a matter of fact, I couldn't read the book because it was not yet printed and translated. But this jacket won several prizes, and so the editor, Roger Straus, met me at a party and said, "We have now a new book coming out, called *The Wayward Wife*. Do you have an idea how we should make its cover?" I closed my eyes and said, "Yes, I see a lonely road and a naked girl on it." He said, "That's a marvelous idea, but where will you get the girl?" I said, "Roger, where will I get the lonely road?" But I got the lonely road, as you can see here, although it was very difficult. But the funny thing was, this picture could not be published in The New York Times. The way The New York Times published it was by putting a circle of type on the girl's body.

### Three projects

I have made many photographs in this vein, but I would like to talk to you now about three of my major projects. One of them started this way: Once, after a show, my wife and I went into the Russian Tea Room and there, suddenly, I met a man whose face I recognized. It was Fernandel, the French comedian, whom I had admired for many, many years. When I found myself so close to him, I shook his hand and asked him what he was doing in New York. He was only here for a few days, then I suddenly realized that we were not acquainted and I took leave. Yvonne, my wife, was with me and since she always inspires me, she started to inspire me again: "You must photograph this man." I said, "All right, but who would publish the pictures? Nobody here knows him yet."

She said, "You'll make him known." I said, "How?" She said, "You'll think of something." I said, "He doesn't even speak a word of English." Suddenly an idea came to me. I would ask him questions and he would answer me only with his facial expressions. That was, at that time, a completely new idea. Pictures with captions were used as long as photography has been known. But to read first a caption and then turn the page and see the picture, this was a thing that was absolutely new, had never been done before, and has since been done so much that nobody even thinks that some photographer by the name of Halsman invented it for the first time.

By the way, when the picturebook *The Baby* came out, Simon and Schuster were good enough to give me two per cent royalty, just because it was my idea. Then came *The Swede, The Comedian, The Secretary, The Legs.* Even legs were used to express their thoughts by their positions, and so on. For example, a question that I asked Fernandel and that I knew would be good for many years, was, "What do you think about the international situation?" Then comes the question that is not the funniest, but it sets the *leitmotif* of the entire book. The interviewer asks, "We Americans are very much against sin. How about you, Monsieur?" This question shows the idea behind the interview, the clash of the American Puritan and the Gallic man of pleasure. You see here that Monsieur thinks about sin, and doesn't want to give it up so easily.

Then one day I went one step forward. The first book was an interview, by an American, of a Frenchman. The next interview was the interview of a surrealist, and the book was thought of as a kind of satire on surrealism and on Dali,

We Americans are very much against sin.
How about you, Monsieur?

Dali: "Surrealism is myself."
(It took Halsman 100 hours to melt Dali's face.)

and on modern art. The way it started was very funny. One day, Dali returned from Spain. He comes, every year, to this country. Suddenly I saw that his moustache had grown two-and-a-half inches, and it was higher than his eyes. You know, there were times when people were more remembered for their whiskers than for their deeds. For instance, who remembers what Barbarossa has done? But everybody knows about his big red beard. There were famous moustaches, like Hitler's, Kaiser Wilhelm's, Stalin's, Chaplin's, but after them followed a terrible moustache-free vacuum. When I saw Dali with his big moustache, I realized that he had become one of the great moustaches of our times. Therefore I decided to photograph him.

When I went to my publishers, Simon and Schuster, I had a contact sheet of these photographs and on the contact envelope was written, "Dali's moustache." Dick Simon said, "What a marvelous title for a book!" I said, "But will Dali permit publishing these pictures?" Simon said, "You try to convince him."

I went to Dali and diplomatically explained to him that there were many books on famous personalities but not one book on Raphael's nose, or Picasso's armpit, and that this was the greatest compliment, if I would make a book not on Dali as a whole, but on his moustache alone. He agreed, of course, and the book was published.

By the way, Dali dedicated it very gallantly to his wife, "For Gala, who is also the angel guardian of my moustache." My dedication is right underneath: "To Yvonne, for whom I shave daily."

The book has something like 30 questions, and I'll go very fast through some of them. It starts like this. "May I ask you a few questions?" and Dali answers, "Yes, but don't try to uncover my secret." I ask, "Why do you wear a moustache?" and Dali says, "In order to pass unobserved." "As usual, I don't follow you. What do you mean?" Dali says, "Like two erect sentries, my mustache defends the entrance to my real self." I asked, "Are two sentries enough?" and he says, "Let's not split hairs."

Another question was, "What is surrealism?" and Dali answers, "Surrealism is myself." In this picture, instead of the melted watch, I melted Dali and this cost me about 100 hours in the dark room to do a job on his face.

Dali as Mona Lisa! In his hand, he's holding two bills of $10,000 each, and an armed guard was sitting in my studio while I was photographing this.

Finally, the last picture in the book: I ask Dali, "I have a hunch I've discovered your secret, Salvadore, are you crazy?" and Dali says, "Me crazy? I'm certainly saner than the man who paid $1.50 for this book."

And now I come to my last book. This book appeared only a few months ago, and it is called *Philippe Halsman's Jump Book*. I wanted to call it *Jumpology*. It's had a very interesting career; it's now in its second edition. Especially in England and in France, the jumping did very well.

*Match* brought out two issues and published close to 28 pages. The French started to photograph people jumping, on television, jumping in newsreels, for the newspapers and magazines, and so on, and there is even a dance called "Jumpologie", with a phonograph record of the same name. I bought this record, and you can hear the Frenchman counting "un, deux, trois — jump!"

Let me start with the book. It describes my discovery that through the jump it is possible to recognize the character of a person. People now often ask me, "Well, what gave you this idea?" Then, with my usual modesty, I say, "Sheer genius, of course." But I'll tell you the truth.

I photographed for NBC many comedians and I made them all jump, just to have them in different positions. One day, I put these pictures together and I suddenly realized that every comedian had jumped in character.

There is Carson, who is feeling so youthful; he's jumping out of his jacket. There is Durante, who looks like a strange bird. There is Garroway, whose show Mr. Weaver has created, completely relaxed; and there is also Milton Berle, who is working hard to make a fool out of himself.

So the next problem was, "Are only comedians revealing their characters, or is everybody?" I found that private people

71

reveal their characters even more easily than comedians, because they are sometimes less artificial.

For instance, there is the jump of Governor Dewey. His outstretched arm is a sign of ambition; he is reaching for something, and one outstretched arm means single-minded ambition. There is Dr. Oppenheimer. After jumping, he asked, "What do you see in my jump?" Since he was a man of science, I couldn't imagine that he was mostly motivated by ambition, and I said, "Maybe you are showing a new road to the universe." Dr. Oppenheimer laughed and said, "No, I was simply reaching for something." So, you see, you cannot escape my rule.

There are the father and son Sarnoff, and these photographs prove that the jump position is hereditary, which sounds silly. But since character is a hereditary trait, it's obvious that the jump will be also similar.

There are the partners, Rodgers and Hammerstein; there are Simon and Schuster. Rodgers is outgoing and Hammerstein was the introvert; Simon is the introvert, Schuster is the extrovert. You see that in successful partnership the partners should be complete opposites. However, you have both partners that jump the same way — as Dean Martin and Jerry Lewis. Of course, their partnership didn't last, and had to break up.

This is the Duchess of Windsor. You know, I am a great believer in Freud, who said that there are no accidents without a subconscious cause, therefore this is a very interesting picture.

Now, coming to the love goddesses of our times, there are Lollobrigida, jumping like a playful girl; Marilyn Monroe, also a playful child; and Brigitte Bardot, also playful, a child, throwing up her feet. Jumpology explains to you that the love goddesses of today have to be child-women. If they were women-women, passionate women, then it would be more difficult for an American male to dream of them, because an American male, even in his dreams, wants to feel at ease. It is much easier to feel superior with a child-woman, like Marilyn Monroe or Brigitte Bardot, than with a woman like Theda Barra, or Garbo or Dietrich. So we realize that today only the child-women have the potential ability to become love goddesses.

*The Duchess of Windsor.*

But some of the people would not jump for me. Of all the people that I have asked, not one woman refused. However, out of 300 jumpers, ten men refused. One was the former President, Herbert Hoover, who told me that for him jumping would be like acting and, since he was not an actor, he would not jump. When I asked the young man, Van Cliburn, to jump, he refused. When I asked why he said, "It doesn't need any explanation," and lifted his chin. At this moment I photographed him.

I found that I had great difficulties with the British. The British are the most seagoing of nations and — possibly because of this — simply refused to jump. Lord Mountbatten said, "How foolish it is to jump," so I didn't even ask him. Aneurin Bevin looked suspiciously at me, when I asked him to jump, and refused. When I photographed Gaitskell, I didn't even have the courage to ask him. When I started to pack my equipment, he said, "You didn't ask me to jump," and, of course, I then asked him. There was at that time a rivalry between Bevin and Gaitskell. Attlee had resigned, and the question was, who would be the leader of the Labor Party. When I saw Gaitskell jumping, I immediately predicted that the dynamic one would become the leader and, of course, I was right.

Then I came to this country from England and had to photograph Governor Harriman, who was fighting for the Democratic nomination. After making my portrait, I asked him to jump. The Governor thought for a moment and said: "In respect to the office that I occupy, I have to refuse." I thought, "The office you hope to occupy." The next month I had to photograph Adlai Stevenson, and I asked him to jump. He jumped and I told him the story about Bevin and Gaitskell and said, "Mr. Stevenson, you will win the nomination." Of course, I was right again.

So, you see, this study of Jumpology will give you the possibility of recognizing people's character, fast and inexpensively. You simply make them jump.

This is the end of my third book. I don't know what will be my fourth book because nobody knows what idea you will have the next day, but I am now at the end of my piece. You remember, the title was, "Am I A Camera?" As you see, I kept my promise not to discuss it, and if you think after this that I am a camera, I'll be very, very flattered; but if you think that I am not a camera I'll be flattered even more.

# The Challenge of Sameness

## CLAUDIO CAMPUZANO

Claudio Campuzano ardently practices international visual communications. Trained as an engineer at the School of Engineering, University of Buenos Aires, Argentina—the country of his birth—he plunged into political and economic journalism. His liberal views made him *persona non grata* to the Peron regime, so he turned to advertising. After the downfall of Peron in 1955 he became press adviser to the Secretary of Commerce and to the Economic Cabinet of the Aramburu administration. His career as a photojournalist began in Rio de Janeiro as a photographer for *Manchete*, one of Brazil's two great picture magazines, free lancing for European publications also. He came to the United States on assignment from *Manchete* to cover the United Nations and as a photographer-writer. He then was New York correspondent for *Visao*, the Brazilian news magazine. Besides *Manchete* and *Visao* his work has appeared frequently in *Life en Espanol*, *Hablemos* and *Vision*. He makes his permanent residence in New York City.

# the challenge of sameness

I HAVEN'T been in the United States long enough to know from personal experience how many times since 1955 the exhibition that the Museum of Modern Art entitled "The Family of Man" has been used as a springboard for speculation on the imaginative uses of photography as a far-reaching medium of visual communication. However, I suspect enough of that has been done; enough, at least, so that its mere mention will evoke in you the agonizing thought that here is yet another man bent on treading this well-traveled road. Let me assure you that this is not so.

If, briefly, I discuss the "Family of Man" exhibition before attempting the analysis of the problems of photography in Latin America, it is because I feel that by first establishing some common ground we will understand each other better. And it is inevitable that, as a photographer, I would want to choose as a term of reference one of the events which served to emphasize, in the words of Edward Steichen, that "the art of photography is a dynamic process of giving form to ideas and of explaining man to man."

"The Family of Man" enjoyed an unusual popularity in Latin America. It was seen and talked of in many places, inside and outside artistic circles and always, as it seemed to me, with that warmth of praise which greets the objectification of strong, contemporary feelings. Presumably, then, "The Family of Man" gave visual pleasure, coupled with the confirmation of a philosophy of life.

I was fortunate enought to be in New York while it was being shown at the Museum of Modern Art. I can still evoke the wonderment and emotion I felt at that time, and I consider it one of my unforgettable experiences. Time has not modified that impression. "The Family of Man" was, and still is now, a momentous statement.

I felt at that time that "The Family of Man" had achieved its objective of showing, as Carl Sandburg said, that "We are alike in all countries and tribes in trying to read what sky, land and sea say to us. Alike and ever alike we are on all continents in the need of love, food, clothing, work, speech, worship, sleep, games, dancing, fun." I don't believe anybody could take issue with this statement.

### A challenge to visual communication

We are alike, yes. There *is* a sameness. But this is only a beginning. Man blends and interweaves his needs, his impulses, his desires, in a myriad of richly complex ways. And as we face that fascinating complexity that is human adventure, we begin to realize that visual communication — photography especially — faces an exciting challenge when trying to uncover that sameness.

A sensitive photographer, faced with the task of portraying the doings of a society that is new to him, may quite readily establish with it an emotional rapport. This emotional rapport will help him in the interpretation of this human group to his audience. Emotional rapport, however, though fundamental in the work of the photographer, is not all. If he is to be successful as a "communicator," he will have to develop, within the limits of his work, a synthesis that is not only *felt* by his audience as an emotion, but that is *understood* as well. It is not enough that the audience be moved by the images captured by the photographer; these images should also convey to the audience comprehension, understanding of the human group involved. The photographer will find these images easy to come by when he is attempting the portrayal of a primitive or semi-primitive society: the essential human characteristics that are common to all men, and that "The Family of Man" so well revealed, will be easily recognized.

Social relationships in a group like this have not yet attained a high degree of complexity. These essential characteristics will still be visible, coming up to the surface here and there,

77

and the photographer, without distorting reality in any way, may still be able to abstract them in the form of emotionally-charged images. He will only have to exercise a sensitive and wise selection of the surrounding reality. The members of his audience are sure to understand these essential characteristics, that will emerge unencumbered, for what they are, and they will be able to relate them to their own essences.

But what happens when the photographer's interest is focused on more complex societies? Latin America may offer a good example. Here, in Latin America, is a human society that might first impress a foreign photographer — usually American or European — as being materially different from his own. If the photographer does not understand to what extent this difference is only material, his role as communicator will be seriously impaired. He will not realize that many of these different social relationships come, in effect, very close to the meaning of those he knows from his own environment.

Not realizing this, he will emphasize the dissimilarities, the contrasts even, imposing through his selection of images his own preconceptions, his own standards, and he will finally fall upon recording the quaint, the picturesque, to the exception of almost anything else.

Let us imagine now that our photographer is more enlightened and more sensitive. While still registering his awareness of the differences, he might still feel an emotional kinship with this human group that he is facing in his work. He will sense that, even across the differences, there are some connecting links, some hidden channels of communication.

But other problems emerge when he faces the task of translating this emotional kinship into images that will convey to his audience understanding together with this feeling.

Latin American society is complex. Its essential character is concealed in and under the framework of a different culture. It is not easy for the photographer to discover how human needs, impulses, desires, similar in their essences to his own, have evolved in this complex society into a different social structure.

Essential character is not self-evident in Latin America as

it might be in a less-developed human group. It can be isolated artificially, of course, by bringing them arbitrarily to the foreground, but this distortion of reality takes place at the expense of vital truth. The photographer will bring understandings to his audience, but the audience will understand a society that does not exist, that has little or nothing to do with the real one. Examples of this are easy to find.

### Distorting reality

Let's take a look at John Q. Photographer. He has just arrived at Sao Paulo. Being a sensitive photographer, he has soon discovered that, although outwardly different, the Sao Paulo businessman is substantially similar to his New York counterpart. John Q. realizes that this is hard to translate in terms of photography unless a good deal of time is devoted to the understanding of the subject. But there is a solution. The subject he picks for his picture story is a Brazilian businessman, who has been trained in the United States, or one who has been close to Americans long enough to absorb their way of doing business. He may not have too much in common with other Brazilian businessmen but John Q. Photographer does not have time enough to really understand the Brazilian businessman.

This happens all the time. Nobody would seriously believe that a writer would be able to grasp any major subject in a few days or even in a few weeks. Curiously enough, the idea that a photographer can come to understand a country or its citizens in a few days, has not been seriously challenged. This has been so, I suspect, because of the success photography has had in maintaining alive two fundamental items of its folklore: namely, that a picture is worth one thousand words and, furthermore, that pictures cannot lie.

Pictures, as we all know, can lie. And as to pictures being worth one thousand words, all I can say as a photographer is that I would not look forward to the task of saying through pictures all I'm saying now. Words have one place in communications; pictures have another.

But if pictures are to play a serious role in communications, particularly in communication between different cultures, some points should be emphasized. The story a photographer brings back when he has been working in an unfamiliar environment depends upon the selection he has made of the surrounding reality. This selection will combine, if it is to be of any value, his emotional attitude towards his subject plus his intellectual understanding of it.

When the photographer has been in contact with his subject long enough, the dialectical process between emotion and intellect urges him to dig deep into the surrounding reality and allows him to come up with a hard core of communicable substance. Such is the way that great photographic works of visual communications, like David Duncan's "Private Life of Pablo Picasso," Eugene Smith's "Spanish Village" or Emil Schultess' "Africa" have taken shape.

The photographer may begin his understanding of the subject he will approach even before he approaches it. But in the case of Latin America, the problem is that knowledge that might lead to understanding is not easy to come by. It is not easy to gain information about Latin America even through the printed word and, in the specific field of photography, difficulties are compounded by the fact that photography is still at an early stage of development in the Southern Hemisphere. Latin America does not yet have a group of photographers, with talent, able and willing to express their continent the way we have seen it happen in the United States or in Europe. Any photographer who has worked in Europe has been influenced, consciously or unconsciously, by the interpretation of Europe by Europeans, and the same is true in the United States.

But the Cartier-Bressons and the Eugene Smiths of Latin America are still to come. Meanwhile, the Latin American photographer has his eyes, by force of necessity, set on the photography that is being done in other continents. Not only because he learns from abroad, but also because he does not have an audience in his own countries.

In all of Latin America, there are only two locally published magazines that make an attempt at picture journalism, and other approaches to creative photography are in their infancy. As a result, the Latin American photographer who has any talent is more concerned with finding outlets for his work outside his continent, either by going abroad or by satisfying the foreign interest in the picturesque from his own country.

There is no sign that this situation will change substantially in the near future. For a long time to come, Latin America will be communicated visually to other countries through the work of foreign photographers, and the chances of Latin America gaining visual knowledge of other countries through the work of Latin American-born photographers are small indeed.

Latin America's visual insight of the rest of the world will go on depending on the work of American and European photographers. Fortunately, some foreign photographers who travel frequently throughout Latin America are beginning to acquire a serious knowledge of this continent.

### How to convey visual understanding

The problem that is more difficult to solve is that of Latin America's visual understanding of the rest of the world and particularly of the United States. Through other channels of communication, Latin America is informed about the United States, undoubtedly more than the United States about Latin America. Unfortunately, much of this knowledge Latin America has about the United States is prejudiced and based on misinformation.

This has to be taken into account by any photographer who is trying to convey a visual understanding of the United States to a Latin American audience. The photographer has to judge to what extent the prejudices and the misinformation of his audience will put an erroneous interpretation upon his work.

If the photographer is guided by an ethical imperative that compels him to search for the truth in his work — and I certainly believe he should — he must be aware of the circumstances that precondition his audience. He may disregard these circumstances and come up with a remarkable work of art, but although much could be said of the impressionistic value of his approach, certainly its value for purposes of communication would be small.

A show of crude, unmitigated sensitivity on the part of the photographer may in some way impress an audience, but if photography is going to achieve some measure of success as a medium of communication, it has to discipline itself to stronger intellectual codes.

Just because I believe it will clarify my statement, I would like you to see a small example of how the photographer should take into account the cultural background of his audience.

In April of 1958, one of the most beloved plays of the Spanish-speaking theatre, "Blood Wedding" by the Andalusian poet, Federico Garcia Lorca, opened in New York. A respected critic, while voicing his enthusiastic approval, cautioned in his review that, although "Blood Wedding" is considered "one of the most notable achievements of the theatre, the elemental passions of its simple village folk, the unrelenting Spanish thinking and the lamentations of its peasant chorus are apt to make it remote and unmoving to a New York audience." Fortunately for everyone concerned, New York audiences found "Blood Wedding" so *close* and *moving*, that several months later it was still running to capacity audiences. *Life* Magazine felt at that time that "Blood Wedding's" success in New York was good material for a picture story in its Spanish edition.

It would not have seemed very difficult, indeed, to convey to a Latin American audience what this success meant: that New Yorkers were feeling the same emotions that Latin Americans had felt before them. The simple statement of fact should have been enough. Some appropriate photographs of the production, some faces in the audience, a group enthusiastically discussing the play during an intermission, should have done it.

But let us first consider what Latin Americans might have in their minds about Garcia Lorca, "Blood Wedding" and the United States. Latin Americans have a sense of ownership about Garcia Lorca. Being close racially and tellurically to the work of this great Spanish poet, they like to believe that nobody can get as close and, least of all, New Yorkers. When we first discussed the assignment at *Life* Magazine, I could almost hear my fellow Latin Americans: "Garcia Lorca in New York? In that cold city of steel and glass? These North Americans will never understand him. It's too fierce and passionate for them, it can never be. They surely must have changed 'Blood Wedding' all over, distorting its meaning and its characters." They would conclude that if Garcia Lorca were successful it must have been at the expense of its best values.

With this in mind, the problem was to convey to Latin American audiences the understanding that Garcia Lorca's play had been successful in New York on its own terms and for the right reasons. Leaving aside the cold, statistical facts of its success, an effort was made to develop a use of photographic images that would convey this feeling. "Blood Wedding" had proved that it could appeal to the emotions of New Yorkers in the same way it had appealed to other peoples, thousands of miles away. Although set in a small Spanish village, the terrible beauty of its conflict is universal. One could almost think of this drama taking place in New York City.

Why not, then, wrench the play away from the stage? Why not play its key scenes against the background of New York City, searching for locations that would convey to Latin Americans the feeling that "Blood Wedding" belonged in New York as much as it belonged to them.

In and around New York "Blood Wedding" weaves its story. The "cold city of glass and steel" — as Latin Americans like to imagine it — is conquered by Garcia Lorca's drama, and we can hope that Latin Americans felt, too, that the fierceness and passion of Garcia Lorca belongs to New Yorkers as much as to them.

I said at the beginning that I believe photography faces an exciting challenge when it tries to uncover the underlying samenesses of different complex societies. I have tried to make it clear that I believe this challenge to be more to our intellect than to our emotions.

Perhaps because it is still feeling the need of asserting itself as a creative medium, photography has overstressed the emotional values. But I believe we photographers have done enough to prove that our heart is in the right place.

What we have now to emphasize is that when we play the role of communicators — and we do this more and more — the intellectual understanding of our subject should have equal footing with our emotional rapport towards it. I hope this approach to the problems of photography in visual communications has not appeared to be too cold and rationalistic. It was not intended that way, but the invitation to prepare

A house at Gramercy Park is the perfect background for the lovers' words:

*"But wherever you go, I go.*
*You're the same. Take a step. Try.*
*Nails of moonlight have fused*
*My waist and your hips".*

The rejected bridegroom and the outcast wife share their isolation among the willowing shapes of the fountain at Fifth Avenue.

Meanwhile, Death chants from the corner of Exchange Place and New Street:

*"I saw them: they'll be here soon; two torrents*
*Still at last among the great boulders,*
*Two men at the horse's feet.*
*Two dead men in the night's splendor".*

"I was a woman burning with desire and your son was a little bit of water from which I hoped for children, land, health . . ." muses the bride as the water plays behind her at the Seagram Building on Park Avenue.

At Trinity Graveyard, the desolate mother cries for her dead son:

*"And of my dreams, I'll make a cold ivory dove*
*that will carry camellias of white frost to the*
*graveyard".*

this article pressed me into making a stop in my work — a hard thing to do for a photographer and a journalist — and urged me into placing some logical order in my thinking about photography, a thing I sadly admit I had not done for some time. For this, I have to thank you.

# Can Sweden Contribute to Better Communications Between Peoples?

## BJORN O. PETERSSON

The creative director of the Annons-Svea Advertising Agency of Stockholm, Sweden, Mr. Petersson studied at the Art Center School in Los Angeles, graduating as a B.P.A. in Advertising after earlier training at the Swedish State School of Arts & Crafts. Most of his professional career has been with Annons-Svea where now as creative director he is responsible for both copy and art. His agency handles food products, tires, light bulbs, Sweden's biggest insurance account and much of the advertising of The Co-operative Wholesale Society of Sweden which represents one-fourth of the country's retail stores. He reports his hobbies as photography and French wines, being a member of The Order of Wine Butlers, but quickly adds "so far only a beginner."

# can sweden contribute to better communications between peoples?

**I** USED to think about America as the land of Albert Einstein and Marilyn Monroe. So I would like to ask you: "What is your conception of Scandinavia or Sweden?" "Is it the land of smörgasbord and no bathing suits?" We all have different images of each other for the simple reason that we know so little.

If you were to visit Sweden — and I hope that will be soon — you will find a country that seems both familiar and strange. And if you were to stay for some time and got to know the language you would find that the people, their happiness, their problems and objectives in life are pretty much like the ones you know from your own home and neighborhood.

Our nation is not rich, but well off. We have not too many millionaires but the standard of living is among the highest in the world. Sweden is a middleway, democratic country with lots of reason to feel gratitude towards history: no war 1914 and no war 1939. As a matter of fact we have not been involved in any martial engagements for the last 151 years.

You may not be familiar with everyday life in Sweden but I am certain that many of you know Ingmar Bergman and his films. Today they are shown in many places over the world. They have caused considerable interest and discussion. Why? Could it be that Ingmar Bergman brings up the right subject at the right time — and the right way, the visual way? People buy ideas. Bergman is offering not only love, passion and entertainment, he also gives his own views on morals and ethics as belonging to modern life.

Now, just to show you where we stand today, let's take a look at some samples of art, handicraft and graphic design in Sweden.

To start with architecture, see what happened in Stockholm—almost the UN building. When a new idea, a new technique and new materials are accepted and you get the original design for free.

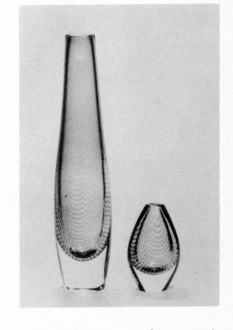

Swedish glass seems to have a magic charm on foreign visitors. Almost too magic. "Will success spoil Swedish glass?" There is reason to worry when we look at the radical approach to glass in Finland. You have the parallel in furniture, where the Danes are close to a world championship. Three months ago my agency moved and redecorated. I am still waiting for my Danish desk. They sell everything to the United States.

You should also know that we have a society with the purpose of promoting good art to the workers and the middleclass. Limited series of signed and numbered lithographs are sold for about 10 dollars each.

Idea communication is a matter of sending and receiving. In the case of Ingmar Bergman you must forgive us for feeling a little bit of national pride, it is so good to be the sending part for once. Being a small nation means we have been wide open for impulses from abroad during the centuries. That goes especially for the time after World War II. We bought anything, good and bad, from the U. S. — Li'l Abner, cars, tape recorders, hot & cool music and movie after movie after movie. You sent and we certainly received. We bought the whole package, the ideas, attitudes, technical progress and business organization, yes even the terminology. In Swedish advertising there are still no other words used as often as the English "art director," "copy," "layout," just to mention a few. I will never forget the tremendous impression created on us by the *Art Directors Annuals*. The only thing I can hope is that you experience a little of that kind when you leaf through *Graphis* or *Modern Publicity*.

But in graphic design we are gradually becoming ourselves and begin to believe in ourselves. Out of that much needed feeling comes new inspiration, accentuated by this Conference and its international theme.

But, to get back to Sweden: we are not actually tops in any particular field. I already said that our standard of living is high. There is a certain respect for quality, taste and design. Industrialization reached Scandinavia comparatively late, so the handicraft has been and still is a strong component in our structure.

Most creative work has a commercial background. The Swedish form is the economic form. A population of seven million people does not allow any big production series if you compare with Germany, England, America or Japan. The economic form is also the functional form. And very often the functional form happens to be the beautiful form. But, so you will not get the wrong impression I hasten to add that there are areas in our business life where you find a chilly creative climate and where design is considered a nuisance. On the other hand you will find strong forces working for taste education, in our government-controlled radio and TV, in newspapers and magazines.

Towards the end of the 1950's the producer's market turned into the consumer's market with sales and price dumping

The new State School of Arts & Crafts has space, resources and an excellent staff of teachers. Stig Lindberg is the head teacher of the ceramic department, a busy man who does not hesitate to tackle anything from pottery to industrial design and graphics.

His TV set with the American picture tube was well received by the consumers, he designs the booklets for his own dinner ware and has even come out with a deck of cards. Stig Lindberg is something of a world citizen with exhibitions in Tokyo, New York and Venice on his list.

Commercial TV is somewhere around the corner in Sweden, so we are not yet skilled in the art of doing TV commercials. But we have movie commercials. as this example for SAJP Tape. They are, as you will see, in the humorous style.

Our advertising standard is fair and it seems that a photo in every ad is a must. Give us five more years and we shall get somewhere. The big handicap is the small number of prospects, with high initial costs, which together make advertising expensive. As a consequence the advertiser feels he must play it safe by "telling the whole story." All of you know what happens, out goes the impact, in comes long and boring copy.

If the ads are tight the posters are not. For some strange reason the clients look differently at the posters, they are more at ease and feel less formal.

Here is just one of many entries to a drawing contest between schools. It tells you that we also keep up an everyday interest for other peoples.

The contest was named "Trade Without Boundaries." It derives from the theme "Without Boundaries" by The Swedish Cooperative Wholesale Society. The Swedish Co-Op, called KF by us, has a permanent aid program for underdeveloped areas. Right now they are establishing a school in Southeast India to train farm instructors who then, in their turn, will help the inhabitants to get the most out of the crops.

as a result. People in Sweden have money, right now. When they buy the necessities — a car and a TV set — it is expected that they will want the quality in things that they have neglected so far. There is a second aspect to a consumer's market: the consumer added influence on production which can mean better function, higher quality.

As I said, we are beginning to find ourselves, to cultivate our own dialect in what is considered the universal visual language. The level of taste is rising, slowly but surely. I am now getting to the point:

*Quality and taste may be the denominators for understanding between peoples. A person or, better, a nation with a mind for quality is intelligent enough to care about others. To react positively to good things and beautiful things is a proof of imagination, the very same imagination it takes to realize that our world can become a better one for all parts if we get to know each other.*

The peace that Sweden has enjoyed for such a long time has made us soft and sensible, with a strong guilty conscience when we hear about poor living conditions in other countries. That is the case particularly when catastrophes hit different parts of the world. The response to pleas for help is overwhelming, especially when the miseries and the victims are shown on television.

The development of visual communications in Scandinavia and all other countries is in the hands of tradition, good or bad. Narrow-minded nationalism prevents the free flow of ideas in both directions. But tradition, in the good meaning of the word, may well be the starting point for communications if it has the power to attract others as a refreshing and interesting dialect in a universal visual language, and provided that it fulfills the requirements of distinctness, beauty and believability.

We are the salesmen of philosophies and goods. Design is just a tool. In our daily work there is always the danger that we concentrate too much on the form of the message instead of both message and form.

It seems that countries arrive at taste and quality education in different ways. These things may even mature by themselves because of the general atmosphere in a country, an atmosphere caused, for example, by religious and geographical conditions.

Scandinavia's situation today is a result mainly of political changes; some call them democratic while others call them socialism. *To us who work there with visual communications the main thing is that there is much activity in the field, the same kind of activity that is behind this Conference.*

# Humor in British Advertising

## MARGARET SWEENEY

Margaret Sweeney, a member of the Council of The Creative Circle of London, is a *rara avis* in the rarefied atmosphere of the Institute of Practicioners in Advertising— she is a free lance art director. London born, "with more than a dash of Irish," she relates, she started her career as a painter. Then, to fill the wartime man shortage, she served in the Central Office of Information as an art director on government publications. Postwar, she spent five years with Colman, Prentis & Varley, Ltd., and was art director for three years in the London office of Young & Rubicam. In 1955 she was elected to the Creative Circle —the first woman to be so honored—and in 1958 to the Council.

# humor in british advertising

**A**NYONE from London will tell you I have an absolutely splendid reputation, not wholly unfortunately, for my advertising or design ability. It's for getting everyone I know in on my problems, getting them to do all the work, and then taking the credit for it. But anyway isn't this good art director practice? Faced with preparing this piece this is how I did it.

I got in some drinks, in the traditional advertising way. Then I got in my friends, the brighter side of them, and turned on the tape recorder. What came off the tape turned into what follows.

I started them all off with the same question: "What do you think characterizes British humor in advertising?". Plante, of Young and Rubicam said, "The pun, visual and verbal."

Berry, of Young and Rubicam, said, "It's the literary tradition. You can't get away from it." (Incidentally, this isn't sponsored by Young and Rubicam, it's just that they happened to talk so much more than the others.)

May, of S. H. Benson's, said, "Humor in advertising is as dead as the Dodo." I suppose this could well be the point of view of the colonial representative of Ogilvy, Benson and Mather. I believe Mr. Ogilvy's "Bible" doesn't like humor.

Gutteridge, of J. Walter Thompson, said, "Whatever it is, there isn't enough of it. If anything can put a bit of color back into the frightened gray of British advertising, I'm all for it."

Now let me tell you something about the background of our humor. Like a lot of things in England, it began a long

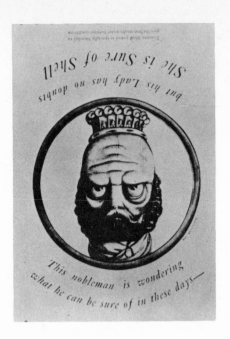

The first use in England of the double take—pre-war Shell advertising. You see it first this way, then it flips over for the pay-off.

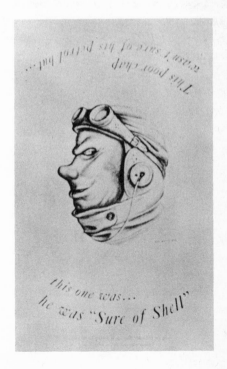

(Left) a campaign based on English place names—splendid visual and verbal puns. (Right) one of the traditional events in British advertising—it's the Shell Valentine.

(Left) Zoo animals have become a Guinness tradition. (Right) a pun on the Guinness slogan "Guinness is good for you."

(Left) Guinness loves Lewis Carroll and have often used Alice in their campaigns. (Right) inventions in Guinness time—1860—the tramcar.

way back. It stems from people like Chaucer, Shakespeare, the Restoration comedies, Lewis Carroll and Edward Lear. Its visual side stems from the sharp wit of the eighteenth century political cartoon to the robustness of the Victorian music hall.

It is true to say that the literary side dominates. We do have a strong literary tradition but, with a few exceptions, we haven't much of a reputation for art. Our humor is insular. We are a close-knit island race and, although we travel abroad, probably more than any other nation, we remain separate and essentially English. Our humor is traditional. We make family jokes, and class jokes on the relationships between us and those above us and those below us and, unless you know the British and how we feel about our class system, a lot can pass you by.

War, strangely enough, has always given an impetus to British humor. It is characteristic of us that we laugh most when things look worst. The family draws closer together, and we joke to keep our spirits up, to show our defiance. It's a sort of "whistling in the dark."

During the last war, there was a big opportunity for the use of humorous advertising. Manufacturers had absolutely nothing to sell, and those who could afford it used humorous campaigns to keep a feeling of happy anticipation for their products.

The Government used humorous campaigns to take the sourness out of the blackout, the facts about food rationing and other nasty little pills they wanted us to swallow.

But it was essentially before the war that most ad men think of as the halcyon days of humor. Advertising was young and, in some ways, immature. In those days buying power was largely in the hands of the top social classes — educated, sophisticated people. Advertising was dominated by brilliant individualists, like Jack Beddington of Shell and Pick of the Underground. They were giants. What they said, went! They didn't have the help of the new advertising sciences, but they didn't suffer creatively from the dead hand of post-war advertising bureaucracy.

It was only after the war, which had been such a leveler of social classes and of buying power, that British advertising began to grow up. We had to realize that we had responsibilities to our clients, and we found this growing up was a painful process. Like most adolescents, we rather lost our sense of humor. It was only quite recently that creative people in British agencies began to use the new tools of advertising instead of letting the tools use them. Now perhaps they are beginning to get their smiles back.

Well, how is humor used today?

It seems to me that humor is used, in those product categories that the public has come to accept as of basically high standard–categories like beer, cigarettes, petrol and bread. The product advantage is marginal, advertising on the basis of "product plus" has very little point and it runs the risk of selling the category as a whole, rather than your own brand. If you can step out front with humor, and the right kind of humor, you can really win.

I don't know how significant it is, but these categories have another characteristic in common: all beer looks alike, especially when you remember that, thank God, we still drink ours out of a barrel. All bread just looks like bread. Petrol, you don't even see! This can lead you on to some interesting ideas. For example, all detergents look alike, and I don't know if anyone in America thinks humor is an idea worth trying out on Proctor and Gamble.

This brings me to women and humor. After all, women are our most important customers. It is said by men, and especially men in Britain, that along with cricket, buying ties, having a sense of humor, these are all things women don't know about. This is a sad outlook and if the Art Directors Club of New York chose their panelist right, at least American men cannot believe this is true!

In the past, women had little time for fun. They were overworked and isolated in their homes, and humor is not a solitary thing. They did the worrying about money, and fear and fun don't go together. They were dominated by men, and humor is born of freedom and not of subjection. But the position of women all over the world is changing and, at least here in America, women are well-educated, they have leisure, they certainly have confidence. Women everywhere are catching up with their American sisters, and when they do they will see the funny side as well as the next man.

(From left to right) *Schweppes invented an entirely new county called Schweppeshire.*

*Advice from Schweppes on how to make a jolly good speech.*

*This quiet, very English tribute to Her Majesty—the traditional Guinness animals pay homage in this Guinness poster at the time of the Coronation.*

It isn't easy to handle humor in a British agency today. We creative people are suffering at the hands of the new committee rule and humorous advertising, even if we have a strong case for using it, like good fruit, it soon loses its bloom if handled by too many people.

You need a singular client, one man, who makes decisions on his own judgment and on yours, who is not content that his advertising shall be just "not wrong" but will stake all on being "divinely right."

There are several advertisers who have done consistently distinguished work in the field of humorous advertising. Shell for example, who along with the more direct selling campaigns, have produced some brilliant "laugh lines." There was the famous punning campaign on British place names, which ran with tremendous success. When the agency decided it was time to change, it had to put it back again, by the demand of the public. The wonderful series of Shell Valentines, surely some of few ads that have always appeared without any product name; in the Valentine tradition, the last line of the verse always reads, "you can be sure of . . . . .".

Guinness is another example. Guinness is a British institution, it's part of The Establishment. It was brewed 250 years before it was ever advertised, and there are drawings of Guinness in the original illustrations to Dickens' *Pickwick Papers*. The Guinness slogan, "Guinness is good for you" wouldn't be acceptable in America, but this splendid piece of self-justification has been running in Britain for thirty-one years. Guinness has a tradition of writing special ads for special positions in a paper. There was a beauty written entirely in Latin, next to the university examination results in *The Times*. They produced at the time of Her Majesty's Coronation a poster to end all posters, with no slogan and no product name — it featured the Guinness animals which have long been the theme of their posters, waving Union Jacks and generally celebrating — the actual glass of Guinness has been swallowed by the ostrich! Everyone in Britain understood and enjoyed this quite, very English tribute, from one of our biggest advertisers to Her Majesty.

You can't talk about humor without thinking of Schweppes. Quite different from the simple direct Guinness humor, it's more sophisticated. It has featured a complete new English county called SCHWEPPESHIRE; in the personalities and traditions of this mythical county, Schweppes parodies the whole of our way of life, and we love it.

[It's a great pity that now this is in print, I cannot show the television work of these advertisers, and others, that I did at the time of the talk. It is interesting to note that these were the most acceptable of all, to the New York audience; perhaps this is because visual rather than verbal humor is more universally understood.]

Perhaps because commercial television has been a newcomer to us in Britain we have been enjoying a honeymoon period for humor. Perhaps it's just because clients know less about television and therefore, up till now, creative people have given more freedom in this new medium. Whichever way it is, humor in British advertising has been given a great boost by television.

I hope that, in spite of the difficulties, when British advertising has learned to take its responsibilities for granted, it will see how its post-war anxieties have killed some of its sparkle. They will remember how they laughed and had courage when they were young. And on the far-sounder foundation of post-war advertising planning, I hope they will sometimes have the courage to make the customer smile.

I think it was King Agog, in the Bible, who said, "He who steps too carefully will find that it availeth him nothing."

## ISMAIL N. MERCHANT

First vice-president of the India America League, an organization for better understanding and cultural exchange between the two countries, Mr. Merchant received his B.A. degree from the University of Bombay, an M.A. in advertising and marketing from New York University. Peter Dunham of the International Department of J. Walter Thompson Co., moderator of the panel discussion, in introducing Mr. Merchant, said he was also "an extremely talented film producer," being the executive producer of the film "Creation of Woman," the first color film to be made in New York based on Hindu mythology.

## DANCE INTERPRETATIONS BY HADASSAH

Hadassah was introduced by Mr. Dunham as "one of the world's foremost interpreters of the dances of the East." Mr. Merchant reported that Hadassah had but recently returned from an extended tour of India and Israel, where her performances were received "with great joy and excitement," with the critics in Bombay and Madras unanimous in their acclaim of her excellence. For her first number, Hadassah presented the traditional dance "Alarippu" in which the dancer dedicates herself to Shiva Natarja, the Lord of Dancers. This is the opening dance in the Bharata Natyam of the South Indian devadassi or temple dancer. Her final number was a satire entitled "Broadway Hindu."

# images of india

**Mr. Merchant**

THE EARLIEST FORM of visual communication in India is, without doubt, the notion that the universe was created and destroyed, in the endless cycles of creation and destruction of life and death, by the King of Dancers, Lord Shiva. In the Judao-Christian world, it was with the Word that the God, Jehovah, created the universe. Did He not say, "Let there be light," and there was light? He merely said, "Let there be," and there was.

Much of this kind of communication in India is through the temples, and dancing. Also, in almost every film there is inevitably a dance sequence of one sort or another; perhaps through this form one becomes aware more readily than through the spoken word.

One of our items in our program is a film on "Mahabalipuram," an ancient Hindu temple in South India, depicting the stories of gods and goddesses, and this is interpreted through the dance. The film is called "Chandalawala."

This gives plastic evidence to the many varied tales and religious precepts, principles of behavior, good and evil — factors which shape or bind our society. They embodied the highest wisdom of the folk. They were communicating or advertising — if you will — a mode of living, a way of life. It is quite evident that the dancer plays an important part in these iconographic images.

From advertising, we pass to traditions, and from tradition we pass to visual communication.

**Hadassah**

Although I am a dancer and cannot express myself very well in words, I must tell you that as an artist and as a human being I am a product of "visual communications-international" — and I do not refer to the title of this Conference.

When I was a very little girl, in my native city of Jerusalem, I was told about religion. I did not understand the words. But when I saw it, when it was communicated to me visually — through posture, gesture, movement and *abhinaya* or expression — only then did I understand it. When matters of soul and spirit are involved, words are finite — stuff of the intellect — but dance and music go way beyond. They are the antennae of our intuition and that portion of ourselves which is imperishable.

This week of April is a very Holy Week for Jews, for Christians and for Moslems. And it was during this week, at the time of my childhood and early youth, that when I looked upon the faces of the Christian pilgrims as they were entering the Street of the Holy Sepulchre I saw that they resembled my grandfather. There was the same expression upon their faces — the same spiritual intensity that transformed the face of my grandfather as he danced before the Ark of the Lord in celebration of the giving of the Books of the Bible on Mt. Sinai — holding in his arms the parchment scroll of the Bible as if it were a pillar of fire leaping upward above his bearded face. And when I watched the Dervishes in their ecstatic dancing, by means of which — in a state of trance their individual souls merged with the Cosmic Soul — they, too, assumed the same posture and expression.

In fact, this movement symbolizing Christ on the Cross, although it is intended to represent "agony," is also assumed by the dancing Dervish when he loses himself in an ecstasy of union with the Cosmos; and when my grandfather danced (he was a Hassidic Rabbi, who believed in worshipping God through devotion and ecstasy and not through the dry, hair-splitting of the intellect) — when he danced before the Lord, he also did this.

So when I became old enough to understand, I knew that "agony" and "ecstasy" are really one and the same.

### "The Fable"*

The dance called "Fable" was inspired by the teachings of Buddha and Gandhi. It is an exposition of the *hasta-mudras* — or hand symbols — the means by which the Hindu dancer

* Script and choreography copyrighted by Hadassah.

"When nobody was so-phisticated" (indicating a well-groomed moustache).

"Soon the dawn came up —and the heavens burst open like a huge golden gate over the Himalayan mountains."

"and drinking of the cool waters."

"and the crocodile came."

"all the birds flying about from tree to tree."

"you are at peace."

tells a story. "Fable" is a dance about "peace and brother-hood" — a condition greatly to be desired but, alas, as yet an unattainable state.

At its premiere before an Indian audience, the dance critic of the *Times of India* reported that "Fable" was "a noble work." It was granted a Certificate of Suitability by the Board for Prior Scrutiny of *Melas, Tamashas and Ras* of Bombay with the notation that it was "suitable for performance or exhibition for public amusement in the State of Bombay provided that the following conditions shall be complied with: — *Conditions*: 'Allowed without any cuts.'"

And in New York, its presentation was characterized by the *New York Times* as "a luminous comment."

A long, long time ago — when nobody, nobody was sophisticated — there lived a great king. The wife of this king was very beautiful. Her face was as radiant as moonbeams and her speech was as sweet as honey, and altogether she was as fragrant as a garland of flowers. They had two handsome children, a little girl and a little boy, who were a joy to behold.

Now this king had many treasures. When his flute player piped on the flute, all those who heard him were intoxicated with the heavenly sound. And the dancing girls — with their long, long hair — were delightful to look upon, and the most graceful in the kingdom.

But alas! In spite of these many possessions, the king was a very sad man.

One night, when everyone was asleep, and the moon was pouring down rays of silver upon the earth, and the stars sparkled like jewels in the vastness of space, the heart of the king was filled with a great longing. So he stole out of the doors of the palace and walked and walked. Soon the dawn came up and the heavens burst open like a huge golden gate over the Himalayan mountains, and the king found himself near a huge forest with many tall trees. At the edge of this forest a river was flowing along on her way to meet the sea. And behold! On the banks of this river — moving about with great dignity — there was a majestic elephant, who was bathing and splashing himself and drinking of the cool waters.

But when the elephant saw the king, he was filled with a great fear. With a voice like a trumpet he called aloud to all his friends. The first one to come was the mighty lion — then came the timid fawn with startled, gentle glances — and the crocodile came — and the pompous peacock proudly showing off his colorful tail, preening his fine feathers and strutting about in self admiration. And all the birds flying about from tree to tree — and flirting, and gossiping and laughing at the well-fed goose waddling lazily towards them. And soon even the fish began to hurry and ripple amid the waves. And finally the leech came — slowly crawling along.

Then the elephant spoke and said, "Oh my friends, let us run and climb up to the mountain top, for I have just seen a man — and man is always drunk with power, and pride, and full of evil and fury. And man always carries a bow and arrow — and he kills! He even kills his fellow man! Quickly — let us climb to the top of the mountain!"

The king, however, did not see the animals. He walked towards a tree, underneath which sat an old man in deep meditation. Slowly, the king approached the old man and, folding his hands reverently as is the custom in India, he said: "Oh man of wisdom, Oh thou great Mahatma. I am a prince with many treasures but in my soul is a great hunger. You are an old man with only a flowering branch as a roof over your head—but you are at peace! Show me the path, I invoke thee—for my spirit leaps like a flame reaching out towards the eternal truths. Why, why does one man kill another? Are we not all brothers?"

And as the king listened in rapture, the ancient prophet spoke:

"Life and Death are one, even as the river and sea are one. The song of the bird, and the thunder of the storm, and the wind sighing through the trees, and the crawling worm, and the tears of the mother, and the laughter of the child, and the lotus opening in ecstasy to the sun:

All these are droplets of water emanating from the pool of eternity. We are all the children—of one father. The heavens and the earth are bountiful. Go forth and teach to all the meaning of compassion, of equality, and of peace."

# Visual Communication
# Through Traveling Exhibits

## ROBERT SIVARD

Robert Sivard is the chief, Exhibits Division of the Information Center Service, United States Information Agency which in many areas is the principal channel of communication between the people of the United States and those of other lands. Mr. Sivard's career has included art direction, mural painting, writing on fine arts and painting. His work has been shown in Galerie Craven, Galerie Charpentier and the American Embassy in Paris, also the Midtown Galleries in New York. He has won prizes from the National Academy and his work is represented in a number of collections throughout the country. He served in the Army in the European Theatre during World War II, being discharged as a captain.

# visual communication through traveling exhibits

A SHORT TIME AGO a Soviet official told Walter Lippmann that "Socialist States will not and do not go to war." At the same time Nikita Khrushchev told him that the U.S. is living "the last years of its greatness." These two statements make very clear that the opposing philosophies in the world today intend to settle their differences not in a nuclear holocaust but rather in a war of ideas.

It is certainly too early for us now to abandon our military defense and put all of the resources thus released into the modalities of transmitting ideas, but it is emphatically *not* too early to assess the potentialities of our means of communication, and the strategy of their use.

The case for visual communication in this struggle is greater today than it has ever been and it is continually growing. Putting aside for the moment *what* we are going to say, let us look at *how* we are going to say it and to whom.

Take the great audience of the Far East — 60 to 80 per cent illiterate — the vigorous new nations on the continent of Africa — again, by and large illiterate. Examine the population of South America, more than half of which is unable to understand the printed word. How can we reach them — through the press which they can't read, through radio and television which require instruments they cannot afford, or will it be through the impact of the various media speaking in a language universally understood?

Let us look at the very heart of the opposition, the communist bloc now comprising almost half of the world's population. We cannot communicate with them effectively except through means they will allow. What are these means? Sporadically, and only lately, have the Communists allowed our radio programs to get through to their people. Our press — newspapers, magazines, books — are allowed in only the faintest trickle, and in some communist countries not at all.

What has been allowed? Cultural performers, orchestras, musicians, and musical plays, and in the Soviet Union, a handful of films. An officially produced picture magazine, *America*, is distributed in 50,000 copies in Russia and a similar number in Poland. But by far the greatest achievements in communication have been through the visual media. Three million Russians saw the American exhibition in Moscow in 1959. Millions in Poland and Yugoslavia have seen our touring exhibit, the "Family of Man." We have shown architecture exhibits, industrial and cultural exhibits widely in the communist world and, even more importantly, they are asking for more.

The cultural agreement signed with the Soviet Union in 1959 called for a broader exchange of films and exhibits. Other communist nations are now evincing an interest in similar agreements for the same kind of exchanges and we must be prepared to supply them.

The government resources presently oriented toward this need are minute. The USIA, the government agency charged with creating the exhibits and much of the other visual media for communicating with the audience overseas, can only handle a small fraction of the task. You and the organizations you represent must seek the outlets, find the opportunities and take the initiative in communicating with this vast audience.

You may well ask how you can go about doing this. You can participate in trade fairs and professional conferences in these areas. You can stimulate exchanges in other ways — exchanges of people, of information and of things. Here is how some organizations have helped through government channels. We send all kinds of exhibits abroad. They range from demonstrations of U.S. achievements in space exploration to exhibits of our finest paintings. We attempt to show how our economy works, and the products of our industry and agriculture, how Americans live and what makes them tick. We call on every conceivable kind of U.S. institution: business,

The "Nation of Nations" exhibit in the Kongresshalle, West Berlin.

The work of Mies Van Der Rohe was the U.S. entry in the architectural section of the "V Bienal of Plastic Arts" held at Sao Paulo, Brazil.

Fashion show in Moscow shaded by George Nelson's plastic umbrellas.

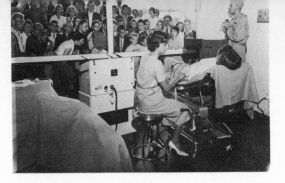

"Medicine, U.S.A." shown in Berlin during the Industrial Fair.

"Rural Development in the United States" shown at the Panjab College of Animal Husbandry, Lahore. Panels describing Pakistan's own efforts to promote rural development, with emphasis on American technical and economic assistance, formed a section of the exhibit.

In Lahore, West Pakistan, the headmistresses of the girls' schools examine a water color of snowy New England from the "Ford Times" exhibit.

Steichen's "Family of Man" exhibition is viewed in Helsinki, Finland.

educational and cultural. By and large, they respond generously. In one project — the U.S. exhibit in Moscow — we figured the cost to these private institutions ran over four million dollars. General Motors sent cars, R.C.A. color television; Circarama, originally made possible by a grant from the Ford Company, was also there. There were hundreds of others — small companies who sent a single product, and patriotic individuals who loaned priceless and irreplaceable paintings and sculpture.

It is only by this kind of cooperative effort, which helps to get across the ideals of our democracy while telling something about our industries and culture, that we are going to be able to communicate effectively with the millions in the new audiences now available to us.

I am sure that the first impressions many of them get will be visual. We should not forget that first impressions are the strongest. We should make sure that these impressions are in our favor.

# The Artist on a Foreign Mission

## ARTHUR T. LOUGEE

Arthur T. Lougee is executive editor and art director of *Ford Times*, the consumer publication of the Ford Motor Company which has set a mark in the use of contemporary American art. Since the magazine was redesigned and revitalized following World War II, it has commissioned and featured for its 1,500,000 readers the work of more than 700 American painters. The collection of original art which has resulted from this program is known as the *Ford Times Collection of American Art*. Mr. Lougee was named "The Art Director of the Year" in 1953. His work on the *Ford Times* was recognized by an honorary degree of Doctor of Fine Arts from Colby College in 1959. He is president of the National Society of Art Directors.

# the artist on a foreign mission

THIS IS in the nature of a sort of "case history," involving industry, government and international communication. During the past dozen years, Ford Motor Company has sponsored an unusual program arising from its use of American art in the consumer publication, *Ford Times*. This publication, with one-and-a-half million circulation, deals largely with America's history, heritage and natural treasures, all assets which are available to enrich the lives of the nation's motorists.

Such broad subject matter has been assigned to American artists, and has inspired paintings which constitute an unprecedented national portrait. The resulting 6,000 paintings, by 700 contemporary artists, have been entered after publication into a permanent company collection called *The Ford Times Collection of American Art*.

From this collection, a program of catalogued traveling exhibitions for Americans has been developed. Over the last three to four years, more than two million citizens have seen selections of original, contemporary U.S. paintings in these exhibits. Last year alone, thirty regularly-available exhibitions were shown, for a period of two to three weeks, in 167 locations representing 40 states, the locations consisting chiefly of colleges and universities, community centers, museums, libraries and schools.

Last year, in addition, twelve special exhibitions of thirty paintings each were assembled and catalogued from this collection for use by U.S.I.A. in its overseas exhibition program. The accompanying reproductions illustrate representative paintings in a typical Ford-USIA exhibit; the caption notes are taken from catalogue information which has been sup-

AUTUMN FOLIAGE IN PENNSYLVANIA, by Robert N. Blair. Near this winding back country road in the mountains of North Central Pennsylvania is Ole Bull State Park, which commemorates the efforts of Norway's great violinist to establish, in 1852, a colony for some of his Norwegian compatriots.

Clay BLUFFS OF BLOCK ISLAND, RHODE ISLAND, by Fred Zimmer. To see this scene, the motorist must take a ferry from Rhode Island or Connecticut. In the late 1800's, Block Island became a fashionable resort, but its popularity declined and the island is once again possessed of the quiet life.

MOUNT KATAHDIN, MAINE, by Maurice Day. This mountain is at the heart of a 200,000 acre wilderness park, given by Percival P. Baxter to his State. Separate from Maine's other State Parks, it is barred to hunting, trapping, airplanes and firearms, but fishing and camping are encouraged.

STONE CITY, IOWA, by John M. Rosenfield. In the 1860's, Stone City was a quarrying center for high-grade limestone. The town faded thereafter until 1932, when Grant Wood, one of America's great artists, established here a summer art colony and today Stone City once more drowses.

TONOPAH, NEVADA, by Gerry Peirce. Motorists traveling north or south on State Highway 8-A pass through Tonopah, the site of the last great mining bonanza in Nevada. Fifty years ago, champagne and plover's eggs were staple diet for its silver-happy millionaires. Hard times have since hit.

SKANEATELES LAKE, NEW YORK, by Ben Eisenstat. The town of Skaneateles is distinguished by a lake at its side, as is seen in this view from Genesee Street. Its name is Indian and means something like "Where the pure water bubbles." Roads encircle the beautiful lake.

BACKROAD EXPLORING IN IDAHO, by Don Bennett. This scene in South Central Idaho may be seen by the motorist who likes side-road exploring. On a stretch of 150 miles of secondary and forest roads, he can find mountains, trout streams, sheep forests and abandoned mines. Nearby is the famed resort, Sun Valley.

SAUK CITY, WISCONSIN, by John Warren. This community, with its twin, Prairie du Sac, lies peacefully along the Wisconsin River. The Sac Indians lived here and nearby fought in the Black Hawk War of 1832. Before that, voyageurs and coureurs de bois explored the waterways of this area. Sauk City has been called the most typically American village.

THE CUMBERLAND PLATEAU, TENNESSEE, by Corydon Bell. This beautiful country originally attracted Thomas Hughes, author of "Tom Brown's School Days," who in 1880 founded the town, Rugby. It was his plan to establish a new Utopia and, for several years, Rugby was all it was supposed to be. Today, it is nearly forgotten.

AN AMERICAN ROAD IN THE SOUTHWEST, by Peter Hurd. Over the years, as motoring breakdowns became fewer and motorists more numerous, a clamor arose for better roads, and the highways that cross America today are the result. When he painted this landscape, Mr. Hurd was thinking of U.S. Highway 70, in Southern New Mexico, against a mountain backdrop.

MT. RAINIER, FROM THE WHITE PASS, WASHINGTON, by Helen Everett. A highway over White Pass, across the Washington Cascades, was first investigated more than one hundred years ago. Soon thereafter, another pass was used and the White Pass route was not started in earnest until 1917. It leads to beautiful high country.

HARBOR ENTRANCE, GRAND MARAIS, MINNESOTA, by Wayne Claxton. The bay of Grand Marais, on Lake Superior, offered shelter to Indians and explorers hundreds of years ago. The town was founded in 1871 on the site of the old harbor and trading post. It was always a fishing center and a port.

GRAND ISLE, LOUISIANA, by *Adolph Kronengold*. This is a scene along the 50-mile "Main Street," which follows Bayou Lafourche to Grand Isle, on the Gulf of Mexico. On the left of the road is the Bayou and far to the left and right are the endless swamps. Whole areas seem to be inhabited by families named Cheramie or Theriot, all related. This is French Louisiana.

MAIN STREET, OSAGE, ARKANSAS, by *Louis Freund*. In Arkansas are to be found houses whose rooms, lean-tos, dog trots and porches were added as the need arose, forming shapes that no architect ever dreamed of. Today, unfortunately, many pioneer cabins are falling into decay, the old stage coach houses have gone and the false-front grocery stores are disappearing.

POND NEAR LIGHTFOOT, VIRGINIA, by *Joseph Cox*. Lightfoot is a village of three houses at the end of sixty miles of dirt road. The village is really only the turning-off place. From there you go into a wilderness of pine, holly and oak until you reach the bridge over the dam and the pond. It glints quietly in the sun, hushed and serene.

DARTMOUTH SKIWAY, NEW HAMPSHIRE, by *David C. Baker*. The lifts and slopes which comprise the Dartmouth Skiway make up a winter sports center for Dartmouth College. Fourteen miles from the campus, five trails have been built and a parking area and warming shelter created, all on a tract of 650 acres, contributed by alumni and local residents. The passing motorist can witness championship meets by prep school and college participants.

NEWPORT HARBOR, CORONA DEL MAR, CALIFORNIA, by *Rex Brandt*. From the level road from Santa Ana, one looks suddenly down on the long, narrow waterway that is Newport Harbor. This harbor is probably the most congested yacht anchorage in the world, with over 5,000 boats registered with the authorities.

THE STRAITS OF MACKINAC BRIDGE, MICHIGAN, by *Edward J. Devlin*. Between lower Michigan and its Upper Peninsula stretches "the bridge that couldn't be built," but which was finished in 1957. Traffic which used to wait for hours for the ferry service now can cross in ten minutes. The bridge is suspended between anchorages for 8,614 feet, the longest in the world.

ASPEN SLOPES IN FALL, ARIZONA, by *Robert Atwood. In mid-October, the high areas of Arizona exhibit a brilliant splash of color on their aspens, maples, oaks and sycamores. Later on, in December, autumn comes again in Arizona in the low-altitude valleys. This painting illustrates the earlier of the two fall seasons as it can be seen on Kendrick Mountain in the San Francisco peaks.*

plied with the exhibits for translation into the languages of the countries which will view them.

This unfolding story of contemporary visual communication involving industry, government and international sharing of art may well interest not only artists and art directors but populations in general. It serves to remind that, while humanistic, or documentary, or regional, or communicating art may not constitute the only valid forms of creativity for the painter, certainly they are among the valid forms. To the great majority of people here and elsewhere, these forms are *the* valid forms, because they fill a great and profound need in people, some artists and critics not to the contrary.

For a long time, the awareness has been growing that America has a vast resource in its artists, almost completely untapped, for purposes of public education and inspiration. As a group, these artists are among the highest-trained professionals in the country, and those who have the interest and ability in dealing as painters with their heritage, environment and human relationships have a fast-growing audience at home.

In their work in the Ford-USIA exhibitions, some of these artists will also have an audience in other lands, and they may well prove to be among the best comprehended and most convincing representatives the United States has sent abroad.

# Audio-Visual Communication

## NORMAN E. SALMONS

Manager of Audio-Visual Service, Eastman Kodak Company, Mr. Salmons came to Eastman in 1945 well versed in photography, having been a lecturer and teacher on the subject as well as an editor of a photographic magazine. Since 1953 he has been in charge of Audio-Visual Service, which is concerned mainly with the planning, production and distribution of Eastman Kodak's Visual Library. He is an authority on the wide-screen, multiple-screen, conventional 35 mm. slides and motion picture media.

# audio-visual communication

**T**HERE IS no doubt that projected photo visuals have become an extremely effective tool in solving many present-day communication problems.

Business and industry, government, the military, general education — all these areas are making more and more use of visual aids in connection with the increased awareness of the need for good communication.

We have come a long, long way since the days of the "illustrated lantern-slide lecture." New tools, the application of new techniques and technological advances have opened new, broad avenues that allow us to lift visual aids out of the "illustrated-lecture" category for *really* effective visual presentations.

One of these tools is the use of wide-screen and multiple-screen images. Although the techniques are applicable to the motion picture medium, our discussion here will be restricted to the "still" audio-visual presentation.

Before we start using the terms wide-screen/multiple-screen, suppose we provide some definitions of what is meant.

*Wide-screen* generally means the projecting of an image with an aspect ratio of somewhere in the order of 2.5:1 on a large screen of similar proportions. The image may consist of subject matter taking up the entire width of the screen or several images occupying halves, thirds, or even smaller proportions of the screen area.

The use of *multiple-screens*, on the other hand, usually involves two or more projectors with the more conventional screen aspect ratios. Images are projected on a series of individual screens lined up side by side. It is also feasible to project images from multiple projectors on the screens designed for "wide-screen" images (see Figure 1). This is a special advantage when projecting three separate transparencies that, together, form a continuous panorama, as shown in Figure 2.

### Why wide-screen?

Suppose we discuss separately each of these two presentation systems. The first question may be, why use a wide-screen format? First of all, it *does* offer something different from the conventional proportions of screen presentations that audiences have been accustomed to for many years. This is cer-

1. *Three individual pictures projected from three separate projectors. Screen size measures 9′ x 21′.*

2. *Three separate slides and three projectors. Transparencies made from one panorama-type negative.*

tainly true regarding non-theatrical presentations that are put on by business, industry and education. The general public, however, has become quite familiar with wide-screen shows insofar as professionally produced entertainment films are concerned. Certainly, such systems as CinemaScope, Todd-AO and Cinerama have made the public conscious of the wide-screen effect.

There is still another and more practical reason for the use of a wide-screen format. Many visual presentations that are sponsored by business and industry travel around the country and are shown in hotel meeting rooms and ballrooms. In many instances, the height of a projected image is affected by the distinct limitations imposed by the low ceilings in the rooms. Rooms with higher ceilings often have ornate chandeliers that hang down and interfere with a large projected image. The wide-screen format provides a means of getting a larger image in terms of width, even with the limitations in height. This is a distinct advantage when making screen presentations to large groups. With screens of conventional proportions, the back row of the audience is often more than the recommended six times the image width from the screen.

Another advantage of the wide-screen format is the flexibility it affords with regard to its physical aspects. We shall discuss this further when we discuss applications.

### Methods of producing a wide-screen format

There are a number of ways to produce visuals in a wide-screen format. Some involve the use of conventional projection equipment, while others require the use of specially designed projectors.

The first and perhaps the simplest way of achieving this effect is through the use of conventional 35mm double-frame slides that have been specially composed and mounted so that they are cropped down from the top and up from the bottom to yield the desired wide-screen proportions. A slight modification of this system involves the use of the "superslide" type of transparency which uses the same cropping techniques at top and bottom. These slides can then be projected with conventional 2" x 2" slide projectors upon a screen having the same proportions as the transparency.

For use in large auditoriums utilizing arc-type 3¼″ x 4″ lantern-slide projectors, the same technique can be applied to the 3¼″ x 4″ slides.

For relatively small audiences of perhaps thirty or less, production of a conventional 35mm single-frame filmstrip can be adapted to the wide-screen idea. In this instance, the transparencies or reflected-light copy can be masked top and bottom during the making of the master filmstrip negative.

Systems making use of special projection equipment usually utilize 35mm film traveling through the projector in a horizontal direction—in other words, the "side-winder" principle. These usually offer the advantage of extremely rapid change from one frame to the next or the ability to provide a "burst" of rapid changes for a series of frames in order to achieve progressive disclosures or a stop-motion effect.

Two possibilities exist with the use of special projection equipment. One is a special projector that accepts 35mm film but projects an image from a film area measuring 24 x 56mm. How these filmstrips are produced is discussed in the next section.

Still another system for using a wide-screen filmstrip involves the masking of the conventional double-frame area as mentioned above. However, instead of this area being made into separate slides, the end result is a filmstrip.

### Preparation of visuals

The preparation of the transparencies in the first two systems outlined above entails nothing more than composing the picture initially to fit the wide-screen ratio to be used and then masking the slide at top and bottom during the slide-binding operation. To achieve the additional width of the film area requires exposing the original transparency in a roll-film camera yielding a picture size of 1⅝″ x 1⅝″, 2¼″ x 2¼″, or 2¼″ x 3¼″. The camera ground glass or finder should be masked carefully to the actual size or proportions of the finished mounted transparency, and the picture composed accordingly.

Wide-screen transparencies can be photographed on 3¼″ x 4¼″ or 4″ x 5″ color film, such as Kodak Ektachrome Film,

3. As with all of the art and photographic illustrations of this article, the original of this beautiful scenic view is in color.

4. These sales training aids would appear on the screen progressively. Left picture with balance of area black, followed by both pictures at the same time.

5. Example of combination of symbolic artwork plus bar graph.

with a similar ground-glass masking technique when 3¼" x 4¼" lantern slides are utilized.

Producing a wide-screen filmstrip for the special wide-screen projector does involve some modification of conventional camera equipment. In general, such filmstrips are produced by preparing the art work or color prints to a standard size and then photographing each piece of copy in the proper sequence on conventional 35mm film. The film-aperature gate is enlarged to the 24 x 56mm image area, and bulk-film magazine is used. This eliminates the need for anamorphic systems for squeezing the image and then spreading it out again in projection.

The other special projector mentioned previously merely entails the masking of the material to be copied during the making of the filmstrip proper.

### Applications

Naturally, the most obvious application of the wide-screen technique involves the use of a scene extending across the entire picture width. (See Figure 3.) Although beautiful scenic views lend themselves admirably to such a format, it is also possible to photograph other locations and situations in order to achieve the "you-are-there" effect. For example, in producing visuals for sales training, it is often desirable to show counter scenes where retail selling is being discussed. Effective photography can achieve the effect of placing the audience on either side of the counter, depending upon the role you are asking them to play. The wide-screen picture does add immeasurably to the "you-are-there" feeling.

While discussing training presentations, we quite naturally think of the next obvious application of the wide screen: Dividing the screen in half; then placing on one half the negative, or "don't-do-this," approach; and on the other half the positive, or "do-it-this-way," approach. (See Figure 4.) The two halves can be placed upon the screen progressively; that is, first make a transparency of the first half and then a second transparency of the second half added to the first. This provides an opportunity to discuss the approach to be presented initially, with the addition of the second approach to follow. This progression of one half followed by the addition of the second half can also be applied to charts, graphs, or other statistical data where direct comparison is required.

127

Still greater flexibility is afforded through the use of symbolic art work or photography on one half, followed by the addition of statistical material or text on the second half, as in Figure 5. Sometimes it is desirable to transpose the order of appearance of such material.

By dividing the screen image into thirds, it is possible to achieve even greater flexibility through the progressive addition of material of all kinds. The progressives can be built up from right to left; from the center to the left and right; from the left and right to the center; and so on, through many variations of these basic treatments. (Figures 6, 7, and 8.)

All the foregoing techniques, of course, can be made even more effective by utilizing either the rapid-frame-change filmstrip projectors or slide projectors with a short slide-changing time cycle.

Another technique is to utilize the entire screen area by adding information to the image already on the screen. In other words, add a text overlay to a background of art (Figures 9 and 10) or photography that is shown first. Applicable, also, is the addition of information to a bar or line graph or pie chart. These transparencies can be produced very effectively at low cost by photographing the art work in reverse order; that is, by arranging the complete layout, utilizing colored paper cutouts, and carefully removing one bit of information at a time while the transparencies are being exposed.

The wide-screen format serves as a medium for providing a relatively large screen image in terms of width, while being adaptable to the limitations often present in "uncontrolled" visual-presentation situations.

The format also provides a certain uniqueness and extreme flexibility for communicating with groups from the screen. Visual impact and variety are obtained by means of the many variations that are possible for projecting the information on the screen.

### Multiple-screen

We have already defined the term multiple-screen as a system of using two or more projectors with the conventional 35mm

6, 7, 8. Series of three sections of art work added progressively.

9, 10. Artwork background at top appears first; followed by lower picture with title overlay added.

11. *Lead title of three-screen presentation "Around the World in 80 Minutes." Wide-screen effect obtained from three separate slides and three projectors.*

double-frame slide screen proportions. The number of projectors utilized depends on the presentation requirements and the physical limitations. For use within the Kodak Company and for presentations around the country to audiences of several hundred people or more, we have been producing two-projector presentations for a number of years. Images from two projectors can be projected on two separate conventional screens or projected side-by-side on one wide screen. In either case, the image size on the screens should be commensurate to the size of the audience.

Here is an example of an actual application of the multiple-screen technique by business. Last year Kodak inaugurated a traveling road-show which made presentations in over 40 cities in the United States. These shows were presented in medium- to large-size auditoriums to audiences ranging from 1,500 to 3,500. The equipment used consisted of three 12' x 12' portable screens with high-efficiency lenticular-screen surfaces. These screens were placed side-by-side and immediately adjacent to one another on the stage. A dressing of black velour framed the top and two ends, while a wider skirt was used across the bottom to conceal the supporting legs. Two 12" strips of the black dressing covered the joint at the two sides of the center screen. Three Kodak Cavalcade Projectors accepting conventional 2" x 2" slides were used. (See Figure 11.) Similar setups with up to five screens and five projectors have been used.

Perhaps the greatest advantage of the use of multiple-screen images can be summed up in one phrase: *flexibility in presentation techniques.* This is achieved through the use of either a variety of images or the repetition of an initial thought on one screen, with the second (or third or more) screen being used for elaboration of this theory or concept. This setup should become clearer when we discuss some of the applications of the multiple-screen technique and offer some concrete examples.

### Methods of producing a multiple-screen format

Basically, the system of producing the final result is extremely simple. It consists in nothing more than throwing an image from each of a series of projectors on a series of screens. In other words, two projectors — two screens; three projectors — three screens, and so on.

Because of the basic simplicity of the system, there is usually no need for special preparation of the visuals. However, special consideration *is* required when planning and story-boarding a screen presentation using the multiple-screen technique. Incidentally, it is not necessary to have images on all the screens all of the time. A complete interplay of images on one, two, three, or more screens can do much to add variety, change of pace and emphasis on certain important points.

Perhaps some comments on the use of vertical, horizontal, and square formats would be in order. Where the array of screens consists of a number of square screens, there is complete flexibility in the use of all three slide formats. Some attention should be paid, however, to a mixture of vertical and horizontal formats that are projected at the same time. For example, a vertical image in the center may be accompanied by a horizontal format on either side, or a horizontal format in the center may be accompanied by a vertical format on either side. Depending upon the composition of the subject matter, other mixtures of vertical and horizontal formats should usually be examined very carefully.

If a single wide screen is used in conjunction with two projectors, it is best to limit the slide format to horizontals only. For example, the use of a wide screen measuring 20′ wide and 7′ high will result in two horizontal 35mm slide images 10′ wide and 7′ high. Using vertical slides with such a screen arrangement and setting up the projectors so that a vertical slide will fit in the 7′ height does limit the size of the projected image so that full utilization is not made of the entire screen surface.

On the other hand, if a series of square screens is used and square transparencies (such as superslides) are produced, very effective use of the screen area results. Not only can large separate images of different subjects be utilized but also a pseudo wide-screen effect is produced by preparing three transparencies of the subject matter so that a continuous, panoramic, wide-screen picture results. (See Figure 2.) Naturally, this is not "true" wide screen, because the continuity of the picture is broken by the black dressing that covers the edges where the left and right screens adjoin the center screen. In general, it is felt that an audience adapts quickly to the use of this technique, the result being somewhat like looking through a wide picture-window.

For simplicity of operation of multiple projectors, it is advisable to couple the projectors electrically so that they are all advanced automatically with a push of a single remote-control button. This, of course, can be accomplished either at the lectern or at the projector stand, as desired. Remote-controlled projectors that accept trays or magazines of slides, such as the Kodak Cavalcade Projector, are easily adapted for this multiple-use technique. An additional advantage of the Cavalcade Projector is the fact that, where it is preferable to have one screen dark, it is not necessary to insert an opaque card in the tray at that point. Merely removing the frame from the tray actuates the projector shutter to a closed position so that a dark screen is easily obtained any time it is desired.

### Applications

Previously, it was stated that the big advantage of the use of multiple screens was the flexibility of techniques possible in the presentations. Perhaps these major points can best be illustrated by some specific examples.

The most obvious use of more than one screen, and therefore the first to come to mind, is the technique of showing a picture of something on one screen while there is a descriptive caption on the second screen. Indeed, variations within this concept are practically endless. For example, a single caption might apply to a series of pictures. In this instance, the caption material remains on one screen while the examples are changed on the other screen. However, where several projectors are wired together so that there is a slide change effected by each push of the remote-control button, it is advisable to have multiple slides of the caption material and merely repeat it as many times as necessary, depending upon the number of slides involved in the progressive series.

Still another use of multiple-screen projection can be tied in

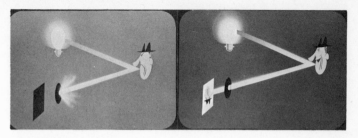

12. *Instructional diagram illustrating incorrect and correct methods. Two separate slides and two projectors.*

13. *Lead title for three-screen, three-projector presentation "Photoscenic America."*

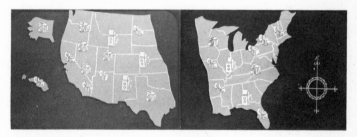

14. *Two-screen, two-projector presentation utilizing split art work of map of U.S.*

with training or other educational materials. Depending upon the effect desired, either the positive or negative approach to a situation might be placed on one screen. After it was discussed, the opposite viewpoint or situation might be added to the second screen. This would give a direct "do" and "don't" comparison, wherein both situations could be viewed at the same time. (See Figure 12.)

There are endless situations similar to this that fit the many requirements of teaching most any subject. For instance, a photograph or piece of art work shows how a certain operation is accomplished, and the accompanying picture shows the finished result.

133

Another technique with multiple screens involves placing a main title or important subtitle across the total width of all the screens. This is accomplished by composing each of the slides in such a way that the words are grouped logically on each screen so that the audience can read directly across. (See Figure 13.)

Another variation of this is text on both screens or the combination of text or title on one screen, and either illustrative or symbolic art work or photography on the other. In order to avoid complications in the registration of the projected material (for example, material to be read across in perfectly straight lines), it is best to space the words deliberately in each slide area so that there is a progressive step-down or step-up of the text material. In general, this usually presents a more attractive composition rather than a single or series of straight-across lines.

There are also instances where art work can be split so as to appear on each screen with some logical break-point in the middle. For instance, a map of the United States might be drawn into two separate segments (Figure 14). Or, for example, in the case of lettering, it is possible to achieve a big emphatic "NO!" by photographing the letter "N" on one slide and the letter "O" and exclamation point on the other. Use a red background for white letters, and the visual impact is equivalent to shouting the word.

Other obvious "splits" might consist of a picture of a product on one screen, with a large price tag on the other arranged in such a manner as to appear to have been fastened to the object.

Combinations and varieties have endless potentials. Art work and photography, art work in combination with art work, photography in combination with photography, text material and art work, text material and photography — all these combinations add up to tremendous flexibility in the field of screen presentations. These ideas are applicable in the fields of education and training; sales promotion; industrial relations; public relations; informational meetings; employee orientation; and many, many others. The sky is the limit. (Wide screen, of course.)

# Visual Communication Through Animation
## A Presentation by Robert Elliott and Raymond Goulding

## INTRODUCTION BY ED GRAHAM, JR.

Together with Ed Graham, Jr., Bob Elliott and Ray Goulding are the principals of Goulding-Elliott-Graham Productions, Inc., known in show business as a "packaging firm." Although no package designers, they do wrap up bundles of wit and levity for their television audiences. Bob and Ray are the creators of the immortal Piel characters, Bert and Harry, with Ed Graham writing down the words of wisdom the two let fall. Bob and Ray both started in the broadcasting business as radio announcers in and around their native Boston, then joined forces in 1946 after each had served a three-year stint in the Army. Ed Graham's writing career began at the age of 16 with publication by the *Saturday Evening Post*, followed by tours, as copywriter, of Mc-Cann-Erickson and Young & Rubicam.

# visual communication through animation

**Mr. Graham:**

I WOULD LIKE to present a film, which has some commercials in it. When Bob and Ray and I were asked to talk here we thought it would be a good opportunity to gather some of the best animated commercials being done around the country — a lot of exciting new things by Stan Freberg and John Hubley and people like that. And, as we got to thinking about it, the commercials of our own seemed so much closer by — John Hubley is up at 72nd Street and Stan is on the Coast.

The best way to present commercials is not just one after another. What you need is the atmosphere of a late movie, to fit that commercial into. And to get you into the proper mood, we have such a late movie for you. It's called "Test Dive Buddies." It was made in 1934, and some of our commercials will appear during this film. (Film screening)

Now, I just want to say that each of the clients on that reel took a chance. And in our business it's a tough thing to do sometimes, to take a chance. And yet some of them ended up very happy with the results.

Other clients have taken similar chances with, say, Maypo Cereal. And there are fantastic results from the wonderful things that are being done in animation — more and more remarkable things all the time. Animation is quite an exciting field.

Now, I would just like to propose that, just as most companies have funds set aside for plant expansion, where they put money into new plants for the future, they should have an idea expansion fund, and put some money each year into testing ideas — which could be flops (we've had some) but they may be hits. And I do think this money going into such a thing would certainly pay off very well.

### Presentation by Bob and Ray

Ray: We had a tape interview that we wanted to put on our CBS program one night. It was all set to go and this "payola" thing blew up and then CBS —

Bob: Oh, I don't know as that really had anything to do with it.

Ray: I think it did and, as long as we have this crowd — we'll re-create this interview with Captain Nils Bartlett, who this coming weekend will be leaving for a trip to the South Pole.

Bob: Captain Bartlett, could you tell us a little about your plans?

Ray: I would be delighted to. We're going to leave Friday. We're going to travel the route that the Cunard people set up, many years ago. You know, they have a saying there at Cunard that half the fun is getting there and we believe that very much.

Bob: I see.

Ray: All our men will be wearing sports jackets developed by the McGregor people, light in weight, keep out all the weather, and will not restrain freedom of —

Bob: Of course, this trip has required a great deal of planning, you've had to outfit your ship and all. In general terms, could you tell us some of the things you have to think of in taking a voyage as long as one to the South Pole?

Ray: Well, you have to think, of course, of food and keeping the morale of the men at a high level. We have three cases of Green Giant Peas, and —

Bob: I know, but —

Ray: The men seem to like these.

Bob: I meant, in general, the —

Ray: Firebrand Marshmallows and many other items like that, we have.

Bob: No, what I meant, really —

Ray: Diamond Walnuts. They keep well refrigerated and on the way —

Bob: Let me get to more specific things.

Ray: We have some Keebler Crackers.

Bob: Now, you're going to leave tomorrow afternoon. You have your ship outfitted, you have the crew ready, and how long do you expect to be gone, and what will you accomplish?

Ray: We'll be back Monday morning.

Bob: I understand. Hope you have a very pleasant voyage and a successful one. When you do come back, where can we —

Ray: You can look me up in the Yellow Pages.

# Artistry and Videotape

## CHARLES A. BLACK

As director of finance of
Ampex Corporation, Charles
A. Black knows at first hand
the dramatic development of
Videotape and its significance
in the communications industry. A native of California, he
makes his home in Redwood
City where the parent plant
of Ampex is located. He is a
graduate of Stanford and the
Harvard Business School. He
spent some time in the now
50th State, and prior to joining Ampex he was for four
years manager of business
operations at Stanford Research Institute.

# artistry and videotape

**F**IVE YEARS AGO, Ampex introduced its first Videotape recorder, at the meeting of the National Association of Broadcasters in Chicago. Since then, more than 600 machines have been produced and placed in operation all over the world. In 1960, there were 50 mobile units carried or even built into trucks and buses. Approximately 90 per cent of the American television audience sees taped television programs, and about 50-million feet of tape is passing through these Ampex TV recorders monthly.

We are making Videotape recorders as fast as we can, and shipping them as fast as we can make them. During the past five years, as I'm sure you know, every branch of the commercial television business has felt their impact: networks, stations, talent, unions, production people and creative people. Because of its favorable factors of cost and versatility, the faithfulness of TV reproduction on tape is a profound challenge to all who are schooled in the techniques and applications of film, particularly in television.

The Videotape recorder was designed for a very specific purpose, that of "freezing" or recording fugitive characteristics of a live television program so that it could be seen in the same form later, reproduced.

As it turns out, the invention has proven to have much broader application and usefulness than we had ever thought. Now, in describing some of the uses of our Videotape recorder, my purpose is not just to report history, nor to tell you how to use it, but to stimulate your own inventiveness. I am cautioned by my daughter, Susan, who was asked to write a paper on Socrates at school. She's 12, and she wrote the following: "Socrates was one of the wisest men who ever lived. He spent most of his time telling other people how they should behave. He was poisoned."

Let me tell you, first, how Ampex and its recorders came about.

### How Ampex began

We are a very young company. We started in 1946, in a garage in California. We started with one sound recorder and, incidentally, Bing Crosby, as many of you know, participated in a unique way in our beginnings.

Bing was in radio for Philco, in our early days. But he had other interests he wanted to attend to, so he convinced Philco he should prepare the weekly program on discs. He tried it, but his Hooper rating dropped, and Philco said, "Come on back, you have to do this live."

Crosby still wanted to find a way to pre-record his show, though, and at about this time he heard of Ampex. So we took our first recorder to Los Angeles for a demonstration. The session was uneventful, and Crosby's people were non-committal. We picked up the recorder and drove the 400 miles home again.

We hadn't been home for very long before Crosby's business manager called: "Bing likes that machine. We'll buy it." We had never figured the price before, but we scrambled around and finally came to $4,000 . . . each . . . for 20 machines . . . with $60,000 needed in advance to finance their production!

Well, Bing *did* take all 20, and I think sold a number of them to the American Broadcasting Company, or to friends and associates. That was our beginning; that was our first order.

We had six engineers in the garage then, but we've since grown to an organization of about 4,500 people. Our sales, in 1950, for example, were around $300,000. In 1960, we will probably do between $60 and $80 millions of business. We have world-wide representation: operations in Switzerland, in England, in Japan, in Australia and elsewhere.

141

From the start we have had a corporate philosophy. We believe in it and have been able to stick to it. Perhaps you'll feel it is rather like your own.

We do not want to be in the mass-production business. Quite the contrary, we are in fact, a very high-value, low-volume job shop. We also have a reverence for quality and precision. Both these policies, of course, are inconsistent with a mass production operation, as far as we are concerned; and it has worked out fine so far.

Price has always been secondary to performance. And performance has always been aimed at the ultimate — helping magnetic recording to qualify for new and different tasks. Maybe this is the reason our equipment, in its simplest form, doesn't get much under $1,000 for a home unit and, typically, gets up closer to $50,000, $75,000 or $100,000 for professional, broadcast or research machines.

### Magnetic tape and other products

I'm going to skip over very quickly some of the uses of Ampex equipment, simply so that you will be aware that the company that makes the Videotape recorder makes a great many other things, and that our depth of engineering skill is not limited to one product. Indeed, it may come as some surprise to you that all of our Videotape recorders and their accessories comprise less than one-quarter of our total sales.

Many of you probably know all about magnetic tape, and the principles of magnetic tape recording, but for those of you who do not, I would like to reduce it to its simplest form, the kind I can understand.

Before coming here, I went to our district office and got a piece of magnetic tape. This is it. Some of you have seen it in rolls. It's coated with a thin smear of iron oxide particles, and we subject them to electrical impulses. The whole thing is done electrically. There is nothing visual: you can't look through it, as some people think. You can't pull it apart. It doesn't ruin it to rumple it, though it's easier to use if it's kept smooth and neatly wound. Its record is contained solely in the varying magnetization of the oxide particles. This piece of tape, right here, represents two seconds of a color television program. It's as simple as that.

Of course, it takes a lot of years, and a lot of work to produce the kinds of results we have achieved today, not only
in sound, but in the capture of visual images on tape, and in
many kinds of electronic instrumentation. The list is long,
but I think you could say anything that can be reduced to
an electrical signal can be recorded on tape. Anything. It
makes no difference whether it's sound, or sight, or acceleration, vibration, temperature change. Anything that can be
converted to an electrical signal — and very few things can't
— can be recorded on magnetic tape.

We make instrumentation recorders that go up in missiles,
that record measurements in outer space, and then reproduce
when they come back into the atmosphere. We make banks
of instrumentation recorders that record up to 250,000 cycles
per second. They are used in telemetry — the radio trans-
mission of measurements. Prearranged material, on tape,
allows these recorders to direct machine tools automatically.

Another branch of our business is feeding computers. I
don't know how many of you are familiar with computers,
but they have real appetites. They can suck in information
at the rate of, say, 90,000 characters per second and they can
spew it out again, after performing computation, at the same
rate. This information transfer, as it's called, is one of the real
tough jobs in computer work.

For instance, we make all the tape transports used in the
Philco Transac, one of the fastest computers in the world.
We make transports for General Electric — and for ERMA
(Electronic Recording Method of Accounting), a special
computer that GE built for Bank of America. We make
machines for National Cash Register, and for Olivetti and
others overseas.

We pioneered stereophonic sound for the home, as most of
you know. That was after developing stereo for theatre systems, to use with films like "Around the World in 80 Days."
We manufacture our own tape and, most important to this
group, we manufacture professional audio and video recording equipment.

### Origin of the Videotape recorder

Specifically about the Videotape recorder now, a sidelight
on exactly how it came about may be interesting to you. Bear

in mind that recording a visual image on tape was not the tricky problem. Others had demonstrated its feasibility long ago. But there is a long, long pull between demonstrating feasibility and getting a piece of commercially usable equipment.

Consider an early TV tape recorder — not ours, by the way. It had only one problem: in order to capture a visual image, you had to run a one-quarter inch width of tape at about 1,500 inches per second, or over 85 miles an hour, reel-to-reel speed. Obviously, this was swell, if you had a big-enough room and a big-enough cartwheel!

At Ampex, we were also poking around in the field. We had, and still have, a fine engineer, Charlie Ginsburg. Charlie had a brilliant idea, but its brilliance was not immediately recognized by his associates. Such an experience has perhaps come to most of us.

Ampex went along with Charlie for a certain length of time but finally, being small, had to say, "Charlie, we have to devote all our energies and people, and money, to the development of instrumentation recorders. This is where the demand is, and we have to meet it. We can't go both ways."

Charlie said, "Well, I understand that," talking with George Long, our president, "but let me do this: don't knock down my engineering mockups, don't junk my equipment, don't clean off my work bench. Leave it there for a couple of months. Let me work weekends, let me work nights, let me talk some of my friends into coming in and working on it too." Ampex, of course, was willing to underwrite this sort of contribution.

Two months later, Charlie had the answer. The tape still had to go 1,500 inches per second — relatively. Ginsburg's solution was to use 2-inch wide tape moving at a convenient 15-inches per second — but swept or recorded crosswise by four synchronized heads rotating at 240 rps. Four heads at 240 rps means 960 sweeps per second. Two-inch tape, 960 sweeps — relative speed over 1,900 inches every second. Leaving some margin at the tape edges, and some allowance for overlap, Ginsburg still had his 1,500 inches per second, comfortably.

That was the beginning of the Videotape recorder. Needless

to say, it got its proper priority for final development thereafter, and we at Ampex are proud of Charlie Ginsburg — just
as we are proud of the "Emmy" award which the Television
Academy of Arts and Sciences bestowed on Ampex for
technical achievement in 1956, the Videotape recorder.

Most people, in advertising or otherwise, seem to regard TV
tape recording as "like live" or "like film." I suppose it depends pretty much on whether your personal experience has
been in live television or in film, but users have discovered
that Videotape recorder is like *both* and, more importantly,
that it has new and unique characteristics all its own.

### The Nixon-Khrushchev debate

For example, neither live nor film could have captured the
18-minute Nixon-Khrushchev debate in Moscow and trans-
ported it as quickly and as clearly into our individual living
rooms. This was perhaps not a particular example of artistry,
but it is an exciting thing to reflect on the powerful impact
that this one 18-minute piece of tape has had on communications and understanding between the U.S. and the U.S.S.R.

The occasion in Moscow was not an accidental affair. Our
producer, Jack Miller, had talked with Vice President Nixon's
press representative, Herb Kline, before Nixon ever went on
the tour. Then, meetings were held in Moscow with the
manager of the American National Exhibition, and it was
arranged to have a Videotape recorder demonstration in the
United States Pavilion, on the Opening Day, when Nixon
was there.

At this time, incidentally, Anastas Mikoyan was expected to
do the honors for Russia. Just as in your business, we won-
dered whether the event would be a smash hit or a flop, or
whether the characters would even show up. When Premier
Khrushchev arrived with Nixon, we really had some work
on our hands.

I'm sure you know of the story of the vigorous debate they
had. We played it back immediately, right there, and Khrushchev was obviously pretty stunned by what he heard and
saw, and by the immediacy of the playback. He wanted to
know whether it would be played in the United States. Yes.
Would it be edited? No. Vice President Nixon assured him
it would be played exactly as he had just seen it. Would a

copy be available, as soon as we could get to another tape machine and make one for release in Russia? Yes.

The tape was flown straight home by Phil Gundy, one of Ampex's vice presidents. Customs and State Department officials were all contacted in advance, and the tape was taken directly to CBS, here in New York, where it was dubbed for the other networks. Ampex arranged to release it simultaneously, so that a scoop would not be involved. Meanwhile, a duplicate tape and a negative kine had been made and were on a plane back to Moscow.

I think it's an interesting story, but what is the significance? Before Nixon left for Moscow, a tentative invitation had been extended to Khrushchev to visit the United States. He had publicly planned to visit Sweden prior to this time but, because of an upwelling of unfavorable public reaction, that trip had been canceled.

Nobody in this country wanted that same sort of thing to occur, yet we didn't know quite how to sample, in one fell swoop, the American public's reaction to Khrushchev and his personality. Nixon had sent up a couple of trial balloons before he left, but the public reaction didn't coalesce one way or the other.

Then came the debate. It hit the papers and the radio and was top news, but the real impact and reaction didn't come until the debate tape was telecast from the Ampex Videotape recorders. It's estimated, by those in a position to know, that the audience that saw this 18-minute tape was one of the largest in the history of modern communications. It was not edited, it was not a radio commentator's version, it was not a newspaper man's report; it was an unfiltered opportunity for both those in Russia and those in the United States to form independent opinions and judgments, from the spontaneous exchange.

Now the public reaction made itself known. The reaction was that Khrushchev was an interesting fellow and that it would be all right to have him over here. In turn, Khrushchev's personal reaction was very favorable. I don't claim I can peek into his mind, but I think he must have had in the back of his head the suspicion that if he could use television to go around what he suspected the government might do for him, he would have a pretty wide audience. And, of course, he did.

When he followed his American trip with a visit to Red China, he commented there in a rather impressed manner about the effectiveness of television and TV tape, and of the life-like saturation of the American public. This was his objective, of course.

It's hard to say exactly what part we had in that debate, and what influence we had in what happened. I think the sophisticates in foreign affairs generally feel that this one incident did a great deal to promote the surge of high-level personal conferences on which we embarked.

### Developments and uses of Videotape

When we're reflecting on TV recording and its successes, we should keep in mind that the technique is not static. I don't think it's even got started.

The pattern we see is one of reduction in the use of photochemical techniques and expansion in the use of electronic and magnetic techniques in television. It may well be that within three to five years film photography will have little or no application in television broadcasting.

Ampex's Videotape equipment design is not static. For example, a thing of great importance to you creative people occurred in Chicago early in 1960 with our introduction of "Inter-Sync," a television signal synchronizer. I won't go into all the details, but most of us feel it is the most important thing that's happened in tape since we introduced the Videotape recorder in 1956.

Inter-Sync permits true electronic editing of the TV tape, creating an opportunity for unlimited special effects in the production of programs and commercials. It practically eliminates cutting and splicing of tape. You can cut, wipe, fade, dissolve — all electronically controlled. You can work from tape to tape, live to tape, film to tape, network program to tape, or tape to any other source with all signals fully synchronized.

I suggested earlier that tape is bringing a challenge to film in the television business. I do not believe that I should tell

147

you the things that tape can do in detail. I'm not a technician. But I have a list of things I want to place before you. I hope a lot of them will stick.

These are things that tape can do, things that cannot be done with film, or that are far faster and more economical with tape: I have mentioned editing and special effects. Miniature settings and pictures can be enlarged to life size, for background. Titles can be cleanly superimposed. Location problems are simplified. Slow motion is feasible down to 50 per cent. Live-action people and pre-animated cartoon characters can be combined in the same sequence.*

All these things are possible. And I won't even go into the tremendous versatility of tape in mobile installations. I read a little note, which I think wraps the whole thing up, and it's this: Tape, on the spot, tells you what you've got, when you've got it. No projection shots, no developing, all the tricks on site. When you do head for home, the scene is not "only in the can," but you've already seen the rushes.

Entertainment production and broadcast is the greatest market for TV tape recording, of course. But education has also capitalized on it.

After the first Sputnik, you will recall, Americans engaged in a process of self-examination regarding our capabilities in the field of science. One conclusion was particularly interesting, and almost contradictory: the *best* natural physicists came from small-town high schools, but the *worst* teachers were found in small-town high schools.

In an attempt to cope with this problem, as many of you early risers know, we have "Continental Classroom," a program that's put on at six or seven o'clock in the morning, by the NBC network, featuring a professor in physics of the University of California. So successful has been this type of educational tape television that they have expanded it and now have a course in chemistry, in color, and other subjects for those of you who still want to get up that early.

Tape also is becoming a key ingredient in teaching German at the University of Texas — and in teaching high school

* For applications of Videotape to television commercials, see *TV Tape Commercials* by Harry Wayne McMahan (Hastings House, 1960).

geometry at Hagerstown, Maryland, where it is sponsored by Ford Foundation funds.

Color recording is of great importance to the future in non-television applications. Surprisingly, the color television camera is the most accurate color-measuring instrument yet devised, and by suitable auxiliary instrumentation may be used with a color TV tape recorder to preserve indefinitely a precise record of events wherein the brilliance and chroma are of paramount importance — as in scientific, medical and military applications. For example, Dr. Seymour Farber, who is head of the American Heart Association, told me one of the interesting things he observed in San Francisco at the last AMA Convention there, when Ampex presented a Videotape color television recording of heart surgery.

He noticed under the hand of the physician an area normally blanked out by shadow, which had not heretofore been visible in any kind of color film. But the electronic miracle of television tape recording picks up exactly what the eye sees. Dr. Farber could see the tissues, the slight blood, everything that the eye could see. This was something we had not been aware of, and he drew it to our attention.

### A look into the future

Now, what of the future? Let me give you a peek into some of the things I think will be coming along here in the field of the Videotape recorder: High-speed duplication of tapes. New and better cameras — and an example of this is the English Marconi camera that Ampex has been distributing for some time. Electronic splicing and electronic editing are with us now: Inter-Sync; remember that name. Here's another one: electronic wave length lighting. Doesn't that send the shivers up and down your spine? Cartridge automatic programming. Smaller, cheaper, more versatile Videotape recorders. Videotape recorders for the home. These things are all on the horizon, and not too far away, some of them. Of course, it won't always be a rose-strewn path. There are plenty of problems that will beset us, and plenty that will be solved. But this is a peek into the future.

I have had a very special reason, of course, for inviting your interest to this Videotape recorder and, more particularly, for inviting you to experiment with it, to challenge it and to invent new uses for it. We, at Ampex, have always had a very lively interest in and a high regard for you in communications and in advertising, the creative end of the business. We recognize that Ampex equipment is about as inanimate as you can get, but it's a link between us. And we realize that our future will be stimulated by your challenges.

As an analogy, typography was nothing until you made something of it. You challenged it, you used it, you developed new variations of it. Type, itself, and the printed word, became something because of the creativeness of the people who used it.

Similarly, radio: Marconi invented it, and Lee DeForest gave it sweep with the invention of the vacuum tube. But it was really Rudy Vallee and the "Chase & Sanborn Hour," and the "Cliquot Club Eskimos" that "made" radio. It was not alone the tube or the electrical impulse. And similarly for television, it's not alone our contribution; it's the type of program that's now showing the way on television, that really is making the medium. It's the personal initiative of you people, combined with our engineering incentive and inventiveness which together will thrust communications across the next great threshold of its development.

# How Far Can You Go With Women?

### HERBERT R. MAYES

In introducing Mr. Mayes, conference director Frank Baker, cited him as "a man whose genius has excited a creative re-birth in the publication field . . . has built great content and presentation in *McCall's* but, more than that, he is offering the American woman an emotional experience, from cover to cover, an escape from the humdrum." Mr. Mayes received his first appointment a full-fledged editor in 1920; then, later, for 20 years, he ran *Good Housekeeping*; now he runs *McCall's*.

### OTTO STORCH

Otto Storch, art director of *McCall's* Magazine, was given in 1960 the Art Directors Club Medal Special Award for "the high standard of creative excellence he has set in his art direction of *McCall's* Magazine." He joined *McCall's* in 1953, and was appointed art director in 1954. He studied at Pratt Institute, Art Students League, Art Associates and The New School for Social Research. He was formerly art editor of *Better Living* Magazine, art director for Jens Rison Design, Inc., and a free lance artist and consulting art director. His work has received numerous awards in the annual Exhibitions of Advertising and Editorial Art and Design of the Art Directors Club of New York, of which he is a member.

# how far can you go with women?

Mr. Mayes

**I**F WE HAVE LEARNED one major lesson this past year in putting out a magazine for women, it is not how far you dare go with them, but, rather, how far you don't dare not to go. The better the typography we offered, the better the general design, the better they speak to this mass audience.

There is, I think, a basic flaw in the current idea of trying to strike an "average" of taste in any field. When you strike an average you are as close to the bottom as you are to the top. And I believe it's the top of the taste we should be shooting for.

We have ventured this theory and tried to put it into practice: that it is possible to be *too expensive* for a mass audience, but you just can't be *too good* for it. We have proved that a mass audience of women will accept the best commercial art that can be produced and that, once given a taste of it, they will be disappointed and let down if more of the same is not forthcoming.

Now, what is the genesis of an editorial feature? In April 1959, I was spending a weekend with Leo Rosten, an editor of *Look* Magazine. We got around to discussing parables and ancient religious fables. At one point he told me about a thief who had become too old to ply his trade. A wealthy man, hearing of the thief's distress, sent him food. Some time later, both the rich man and the thief died, and on the same day. The trial of the rich man occurred first, in the Heavenly Court. He was found wanting and sentenced to Purgatory. Just as he was about to enter Purgatory, an Angel came hurrying up and summoned him back to the Court where he learned that his sentence had been reversed. It seems the thief he had befriended on earth had stolen the list of the rich man's iniquities.

I have a fondness for that sort of fable, and I asked Mr. Rosten if he would get together five or six ancient parables representing various faiths; that I would like to have them for the magazine. After about six months had passed Mr. Rosten came up with the parables, which I then turned over to Otto Storch, and he'll now tell you what he did.

**Mr. Storch**

When Mr. Mayes suggested these parables, photography seemed to be the right choice, because these pictures need a dramatic realism. We selected photographer Art Kane because we did not want to have a lot of props in the pictures, but a simple, dramatic statement, illustrating each parable.

For those of you who are interested, all the shots were taken on either 35mm or 2¼ film, and we made 8 x 10 duplicate prints for performing the reproductions.

Despite the spirit of subject, the preparation of this work was not without its humor and interesting background detail.

Now from the sublime to the sexy. Will Rogers once said he never expected to see the day when girls would get sunburned in the places they do now — and that was thirty years ago. Some months back, we decided bathing suits would be the subject for the coming June. Our fashion editor studied the market and brought together the suits. Then the project was turned over to us in the Art Department.

As always we were photographing out of season, and we decided we didn't want typical location pictures, but preferred to give our bathing suit section a very special look.

Photographer Jerry Schatzberg had been experimenting with a water effect and we thought it would be a good idea to use this with the bathing suits, to get an underwater feeling.

# The wisdom of John *Christian*

When the beloved apostle John was getting on in years, his disciples would sit in a circle before him each morning and hear from him a sermon about the life and the teachings of Christ. Then the disciples would venture forth to preach the gospel, one by one, wherever they could find men to listen.

Each day, the young disciples drew from John's words some central thought; and each day, they set out, seeking converts, and built their message around the thought that John had given them. Year by year, they spread the word, and saw the faithful multiply.

One day, it is said, a group of new and eager disciples came to John, and asked, "What truth do you give us now to carry to the people?"

John was silent for a while, and the young men waited expectantly. At last John spoke: "Tell the people this: 'Children, love ye one another.'"

Disappointment clouded the faces of the young disciples, and they regarded one another unhappily.

"Why do you look disappointed?" asked John.

"We have told the people this before," remarked one disciple.

"We have preached love again and again," said another.

"Can you not give us something new?" implored a third.

John shook his head. "No. Now and always—as old as it will always be new—tell men our Savior's true message: 'Children, love ye one another.'"

*A McCall's Portfolio of Five Stories from Five Faiths by Leo Rosten*

Wisdom is found in many places—in books and in legends and in sacred writings.

My favorite fragments of truth are to be found in parables—tales that have a meaning and a point a moral. So many of them have come down to us through the centuries, so bright and fresh now as the day when they first were told.

Here I have chosen five parables that seem to me to capture the essence of five great traditions: Christian, Confucian, Moslem, Hebrew, and Buddhist. Each culture has its own style of thought, each people its own ethos, each faith its unique atmosphere. And because what is merely different often strikes us as peculiar, I have adapted these stories most freely—condensing, rewriting, restructuring the material so that it tells into which we of the West are so fond.

*Photographs for McCall's by Art Kane*

Photographer Art Kane says his biggest problem on the shot for the Christianity parable was finding a suitable surface on which to write the text. He found a bright yellow fence with great visual appeal, but it enclosed a Government "restricted area" and had a large sign forbidding photographs. Art, in a courageous mood, chalked "Children, Love Ye One Another" on the fence and started taking pictures. Then an armed guard came out and asked him what he was up to. Art pointed to the text. The guard replied, "Jesus Saves," and walked away.

The model in our Confucian picture is Harry Lowe, an actor now appearing in the "Flower Drum Song." We got the proper costume with the help of some old men in Chinatown who performed with the old Chinese Opera Company. None spoke English. I will leave it to your imagination to figure out how this art direction was accomplished!

It was mid-January when we photographed the Moslem illustration. We had to have the magnitude of the ocean to create the right effect, so Art flew down to Florida. His arrival in Miami coincided with the first day of the coldest week in the history of the state. Came shooting time and the temperature had dropped to 36°. It was 38° here in New York.

We found the model for the Hebrew parable only after searching through many synagogues in New York's lower East Side. He is a very old Rabbi living the final years of his life in an old age home for learned men, "The House of Sages." These men spend their days reading from the Great Books of their faith. It is just this action that Art photographed.

This photograph for the Buddhist parable was probably the most difficult one to cast. It seemed that every model we thought was right turned out to be highly superstitious. Some were afraid of participating in a story involving the death of a child. Others would not permit a caste mark on their forehead. The girl we finally used is a receptionist with a New York photography studio. She's the real thing, sari and all. When glycerine was applied to her eye to simulate a tear, she actually began to cry. The tear in the photo is genuine.

Shower in the Sert Room. Storch reconstructs the filming of the bathing suit section to appear in McCall's by demonstrating how the "underwater" effect was achieved by photographing through a rain curtain. For the models, it was an indoor April shower.

(Opposite page) As the readers of McCall's saw the underwater presentation of swim suits in the June issue. The section consisted of four double-page spreads in color. The section opened with a single submerged figure floating off the edges of the paper, the caption reading: "The prettiest girls on the beach this summer will be wearing Precious Little."

## These, we believe, are the bare essentials

Stripped down to its fashion fundamentals, the bathing-suit picture is bold and bright. Most revealing new trends are: The **skin-tight maillot**, looking for all the world as though it were painted on. The maillot, we say, knows no rigid age limits but requires a notably slender figure. The **audacious bikini**, the number-one conversation maker, should be worn, we believe, by the blood-young, supershapely, coolly confident only. Newest version has an adjustment feature that allows more or a little less exposure. The **cut-down back, the cut-out waistline** give a feeling of bareness to more conservative swimsuits.

**The indispensable coverup:** A next-to-nothing bathing suit, we maintain, is for the water's edge only. If you're venturing even as far as the hot-dog stand, you'll need a topper or jacket, often made to match the suit. **The siren colors:** Our favorite shades of the season are the elegant acid greens and yellows, the immodest violets, and, for the subtlest mermaids, the taupe-to-brown range. **The native prints:** Fruit and flower and leaf patterns, Hawaii- and South-Sea-inspired, give minimal suits an exotically feminine feeling. We like these particularly when the suit has a suggestion of a sarong drape. **The head-to-foot look:** We enthusiastically underwrite the color-coordinated bathing costume, with coverup, cap, beach shoes geared to the suit itself. **The captivating cap:** Precious-little suits demand precious-little millinery — and the choice today is wider than ever. The prettiest versions are covered with flowers; highest new fashion, the peaked, pointed-head cap.

*Next to nothing: the bold bikini*

*Next to nothing: the molded maillot*

*Precious little, emerald-cut*     *Precious little, fourteen-carat*

# Index

# Index